MANUEL DE FALLA

GARLAND COMPOSER
RESOURCE MANUALS
(Vol. 4)

GARLAND REFERENCE LIBRARY
OF THE HUMANITIES
(Vol. 561)

Volume 4

Garland Composer
Resource Manuals

General Editor:
Guy A. Marco

MANUEL DE FALLA
A Bibliography and Research Guide

Gilbert Chase
Andrew Budwig

GARLAND PUBLISHING, INC. · NEW YORK AND LONDON
1986

Library of Congress Cataloging-in-Publication Data
Chase, Gilbert, 1906–
Manuel de Falla : a bibliography and research guide.

(Garland composer resource manuals ; v. 4) (Garland
reference library of the humanities ; v. 561)
Includes discographies and indexes.
1. Falla, Manuel de, 1876–1946—Bibliography.
I. Budwig, Andrew, 1954–   . II. Title.
III. Series. IV. Series: Garland reference library of
the humanities ; v. 561.
ML134.F18C5   1986   016.78′092′4   84-48406
ISBN 0-8240-8785-2 (alk. paper)

Printed on acid-free, 250-year-life paper
Manufactured in the United States of America

GARLAND
COMPOSER RESOURCE MANUALS

In response to the growing need for bibliographic guidance to the vast literature on significant composers, Garland is publishing an extensive series of Resource Manuals. It is expected that this series, which will appear over a ten-year period, will encompass more than a hundred composers; they will represent Western musical tradition from the Renaissance to recent times.

Each Resource Manual will offer a selective, annotated list of writings—in all European languages—about one or more composers. There will also be lists of works by the composers, unless these are available elsewhere. Biographical sketches and guides to library resources, organizations, and specialists will be presented. As appropriate to the individual composers, there will be maps, photographs or other illustrative matter, and glossaries and indexes of various sorts. These volumes are being compiled by musical and bibliographical specialists, under the general editorial direction of Dr. Guy A. Marco.

CONTENTS

FOREWORD

As the senior partner in this volume in the Garland
Composer Resource Manuals dealing with the Spanish
composer Manuel de Falla, it is my privilege to inform
the readers that the main body of the work has been
done by my younger colleague, Andrew Budwig, who is
now the leading American scholar on the life and work
of Falla. He was born in El Paso, Texas, and has
spoken Spanish since early childhood. In 1972 he en-
rolled at Stanford University, where he began his study
of the classic Hispanic guitar. By the time he trans-
ferred to the University of Chicago in 1975, he had
formed a deep rapport with the music of Manuel de Falla.

He continued his graduate work at the University of
Chicago, where he studied music theory and piano under
the direction of Easley Blackwood and completed his
Masters Degree in Music History and Theory. As no
members of the music faculty had any direct connection
with Hispanic music, Professor Robert P. Morgan, head
of the Department of Music, asked me if I would be
willing to undertake the task of working with Budwig's
dissertation, "Manuel de Falla's *Atlántida*: An Historical and Analytical Study." I was indeed very pleased
to do so. The dissertation defense, on May 4, 1984--
involving a four-hundred-page presentation--was total-
ly approved.

Meanwhile, Budwig and his wife Judith had spent a
year in Spain on a grant from the Fulbright Commission,
beginning in September of 1981. I had put him in
touch with Falla's niece, María Isabel de Falla de
Paredes, who had dedicated herself to making widely

known the entire life and work of Manuel de Falla. She gave Budwig complete access to all the available material on Falla, both in Cordoba and Madrid.

When I first made contact with Garland Publishing, I proposed Manuel de Falla as a subject for their Resource Manuals and included Andrew Budwig as my co-partner. My readers, I believe, will be grateful for that choice.

Gilbert Chase

PREFACE

Manuel de Falla is generally considered the greatest
Spanish composer since the Golden Age of Victoria,
Morales, and Cabezón. His orchestral suites are part
of the standard symphonic repertory and his folk song
arrangements are still quite popular. In addition to
being an outstanding musician, Falla was a driving
force in the Spanish *Generación de '27*, a group of
young artists and writers that included Picasso,
Lorca, and Dalí.

Much of what has been written about Falla has little or no basis in fact. As a young man growing up in
Cadiz, Falla is said to have been a quiet, devout soul
who loved to play the piano and write plays. As Falla
matured and began to gain recognition he spent much
effort protecting his privacy and that of his family. The primary purpose of this book is to provide
the reader with substantial information about Falla's
life and works. Although every effort has been made
to consult primary sources, such as the unpublished
autographs and correspondence in the family archives,
when factual information on his life or works is
unattainable, references have been selected so as to
offer a broad spectrum of reliable views.

The biography in this book is intended for Falla
researchers and casual readers alike. It is not a
survey of his life and works but rather a selective
examination of Falla's periods of greatest crisis and
creativity. Although this biography is far from
comprehensive, it does point out the errors and con-
tradictions in the standard biographies which have
given rise to misconceptions about Falla.

The chronological list of Falla's works is the first complete catalog of every known composition and musical arrangement. Items include dates of composition and performance, descriptions, location of manuscripts, and other pertinent information.

The bibliographic chapters are arranged in order of importance: major books, articles, and references to Falla are followed by articles on specific works. The final chapters should prove helpful to anyone looking for information on Falla's personal life since they contain references to his writings, correspondence in books or collections, and tributes to Falla. Obscure items that might shed some light on problems in Falla research have been included; many of these items are merely newspaper articles, but articles that Falla himself felt were important enough to save in his personal files. All annotations are based on an examination of the items themselves and many provide suggestions for lines of research.

The bibliographies in the standard Falla biographies as well as those in *RILM Abstracts*, *Music Index*, and *The Music of Spain* have been useful in forming a basis for selection. Many of the lesser-known items have been drawn from the bibliographies of my dissertation on Falla's *Atlántida* and articles on *Atlántida* and *The Three-Cornered Hat*. Many books and articles cited were discovered in the archives of the Falla family, and I am deeply indebted to María Isabel de Falla for granting me access to her private library.

To Mrs. Falla, the composer's niece, and to her husband, Jose García de Paredes, I owe my thanks and appreciation. I would also like to acknowledge Ramón Bela and Patricia Zahneser of the Spanish Fulbright office for their assistance during my year as a doctoral research fellow in Madrid. To my friends Professor Roger Utt (The University of Chicago), Rodolfo Villalobos, Jeffery Dean, and Mary Paquette-Abt, and to my loving and understanding wife Judith, I owe my gratitude for encouragement.

Finally, I owe special thanks to my mentor and collaborator Gilbert Chase, without whom none of my work on Falla would have been possible. Dr. Chase and

Dr. Guy Marco, general editor of the Garland Composer Series, transformed my jumbled, dog-eared manuscripts into an organized, comprehensible book. I am grateful for their help and patience.

Andrew Budwig
The University of the South
September 1985

Falla's mother, María Jesusa Matheu Zavala.

Falla's father, José María de Falla Franco.

Falla and his gypsy "nanny," La Morilla--The Moor.

Falla in Cadiz, age 14 (1890).

Falla with Leonide Massine in the Patio of the
Lions, Alhambra Palace (1916).

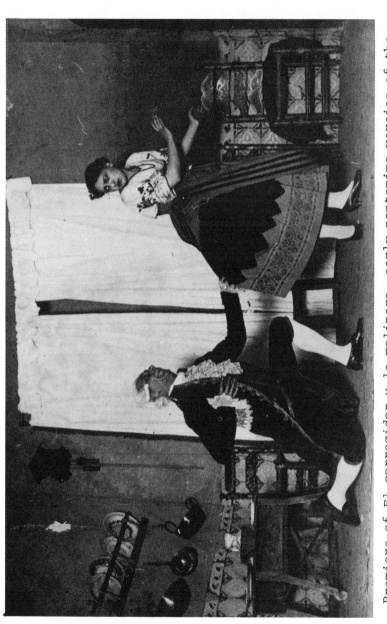

Premiere of *El corregidor y la molinera*, early pantomime version of the ballet *The Three-Cornered Hat* (1916).

Francisco García Lorca, Antonio Luna, María del Carmen de Falla, Federico García Lorca, Wanda Landowska, Manuel de Falla, José Segura (1922).

Falla in a Parisian cafe, hours before the premiere of *El retablo* (1923).

Recording the *Harpsicord Concerto*, Salle Pleyel, Paris (1927).

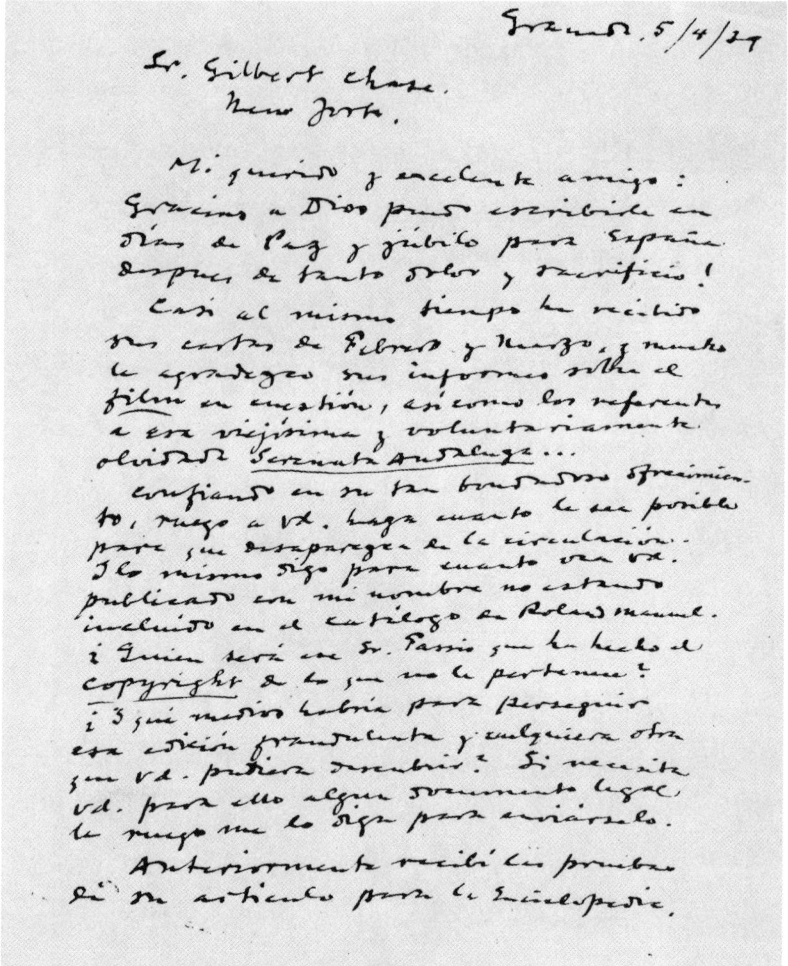

Granada. 5/4/39

Sr. Gilbert Chase.
New York.

Mi querido y excelente amigo:
Gracias a Dios puedo escribirle en días de Paz y júbilo para España después de tanto dolor y sacrificio!

Casi al mismo tiempo he recibido sus cartas de Febrero y Marzo, y mucho le agradezco sus informes sobre el film en cuestión, así como los referentes a esa viejísima y voluntariamente olvidada Serenata Andaluza...

Confiando en su tan bondadoso ofrecimiento, ruego a Vd. haga cuanto le sea posible para que desaparezca de la circulación. Y lo mismo digo para cuanto vea Vd. publicado con mi nombre no estando incluido en el catálogo de Roland Manuel.
¿Quién será ese Sr. Farrio que ha hecho el copyright de lo que no le pertenece?
¿Y qué medios habría para perseguir esa edición fraudulenta y cualquiera otra que Vd. pudiera descubrir? Si necesita Vd. para ello algún documento legal, le ruego me lo diga para enviárselo.

Anteriormente recibí las pruebas de su artículo para la Enciclopedia.

Two-page letter to Gilbert Chase (1929).

en el que tanto honor me hace Vd. y que muchísimo le agradezco...

Cuando lo recibí tenía todo mi tiempo acaparado por unas notas sobre Ravel para la _Revue Musicale_, y por eso no he podido aún terminar las correcciones que Vd. tan amablemente me pide.

Se las mandaré muy pronto y por correo aéreo de ser posible. No lo hago ahora, como quisiera, porque la emoción que todos sentimos por la Paz y la liberación total de los pueblos de España que aún sufrían martirio y cautiverio, ha coincidido con un retroceso en mi curación. Pero ruego a Vd. que haga por aplazar la publicación de su artículo, pues sería lástima que apareciera sin las correcciones.

En cuanto a las cuatro _Piezas Españolas_, es cierto que las empecé a componer en Madrid, pero las terminé en París poco antes de ser publicadas. Durand me las pidió por indicación de Debussy, Dukas y Ravel, que tuvieron la gran generosidad de interesarse espontáneamente por ellas.

Los informes que Vd. me pide en su carta del 21 Febr° procuraré con todo interés obtenerlos por el Ministerio de Educación...

Con agradecimiento reiterado le envía un cordialísimo saludo su muy amigo

Manuel de Falla

Trip to the Alpujarias, near Granada (1932).

Trip to Sierra Nevada near Granada (1932).

Inscribed photo to Gilbert Chase (1933).

Falla in his home in Granada.

Falla in Buenos Aires (1940).

Manuel de Falla

CHAPTER I

A PORTRAIT OF MANUEL DE FALLA
by Andrew Budwig

One hears much about some sort of ballet or song
that [the painter José María] Sert is doing with
Falla for the Spanish court. It is said that [the
director Max] Reinhardt is most interested, ...
It was a young Catalan painter who sees a lot of
Sert that told me this, obfuscating his account
with the thousands of mysteries of which the Spaniards are so fond.[1]

If, as Darius Milhaud contended, the Spanish are
a mysterious lot, then no Spaniard could have been more
Spanish than Manuel de Falla (1876-1946). In order to
dispel the myths that surround this great artist one
must delve into his musical autographs, his correspondence, and even the press clippings he saved. Although
a few of Falla's biographers have contributed to our
understanding of his personality by sharing their own
experiences and correspondence with us, none has at-
tempted to synthesize the vast quantity of *published*
primary sources into a unified characterization of
Falla. In addition to presenting new documents here,
I shall describe the composer as I have come to know
him through published material and through the letters
and musical sketches housed in the Falla family archives in Madrid.[2] This biographical portrait com-
prises four sections, each of which focuses on a critical period in Falla's artistic development: his youth
(1876-1900), his Paris years (1907-14), the period in
which he worked on *The Three-Cornered Hat* (1916-19),

and the epoch of the Second Republic (1931-36).

Falla's Youth (1876-1900)

An intense spirituality and asceticism character-
ize the life and work of Manuel de Falla. By the age
of eleven he had already made a name for himself in
Cadiz by performing Haydn's *Seven Last Words of Christ*
on the piano with his mother and by rendering an excel-
lent watercolor copy of a pre-Raphaelite Virgin and
Child.[3] Juan Viniegra y Lasso, a childhood friend of
Falla, is the most reliable contemporary source for
information about the composer's parents.[4] José María
Falla descended from a family of Valencian merchants
whose trade brought them to the Atlantic seaport of
Cadiz. María Jesusa Matheu, who was of Catalan ancestry, was more cultured than her husband and is said to
have been a talented pianist. According to Viniegra[5]
and Manuel Orozco,[6] who came to know Falla in Granada
(1920-39), the sensitive young boy received his first
instruction in music and letters from his mother and
from his maternal grandfather, Manuel Matheu y Parodi,
for whom he was named. Padre Francisco Paula de
Fedriani, the priest entrusted with the religious education of a dozen or so wealthy sons of Cadiz, assumed
the role of advisor to Falla when his grandfather died
on 28 April 1884.

Manuel de Falla y Matheu was born in Cadiz on 23
November 1876, the first of five children, of whom only
three survived beyond infancy. María del Carmen, five
years younger than Manuel, became his lifelong companion in 1920 after the death of their mother and father;
Germán, twelve years his brother's junior, never developed close ties with Manuel because of differences in
ages and interests: Germán spent much of his adult life
working as an architect in Guatemala and the United
States.

The first document one normally consults when
looking for information about someone's ancestry is a
baptismal certificate. Strange as it seems, none of
Manuel de Falla's biographers have transcribed this
document, reproduced by Viniegra:[7]

In the city of Cadiz, capital of its province and
bishopric, on 26 November 1876, I, Don Manuel
Marañón, the godfather, by the authority of this
parish, solemnly baptize Manuel, María de los
Dolores, Clemente,[8] Ramón del Sagrado Corazón de
Jesús, who was born the 23rd day of this month
at six in the morning of Don José María Falla and
Doña María Jesusa Matheu, natives of Cadiz, mar-
ried in [the parish of] San Antonio: paternal
grandparents Don Francisco de Falla and Doña María
Dolores Franco, natives of Cadiz; maternal grandparents, Don Manuel [Matheu y Parodi], native of
Cadiz, and Doña María Jesusa García, native of
Guatemala; godparents, the maternal grandfather
and [the maternal aunt] Doña Magdalena Parodi,
advised of their obligations. Witnessed by Don
Francisco Falla and Doña Jesusa Matheu. And
signed so that it be put in effect, ut supra.
                          (signed) Manuel Pérez Marañón

The predominance of the maternal side of Falla's
family in this document is noteworthy. Two of his
names, Manuel and Clemente, were given by members of
his mother's family whose surname, Matheu y Parodi,
reveals a Catalan and Italian ancestry. His godmother,
Magdalena, was the sister of his maternal grandmother,
who came from a wealthy Guatemalan family. Viniegra
states that María Jesusa's parents fiercely opposed
her marriage to José Falla, but when they realized the
union was inevitable they offered the generous sum of
400,000 pesetas (about $80,000) as a dowry.[9]
    Another document that contains important informa-
tion about Falla's upbringing is his will, which has
been transcribed by Campoamor Gonzáles.[10] In this tes-
tament Falla carefully specified which of his relatives
and music teachers were to have special prayers said
to their memory after his death. Among the teachers
mentioned are his mother, Clemente Parodi, and Eloisa
Galluzzo, a pious woman who, it is said, abandoned her
career in music to become a nun.
    Photographs of the young Manuel de Falla portray
a frail, sensitive child costumed as a bullfighter,
and later, as a solemn Don Juan.[11] His parents

subscribed to the lavishly illustrated periodicals of the day,[12] and as a result, the six-year-old Manuel took to writing and illustrating his own monthly magazines: *The Rattle-Brain*, *The Buffoon*, and *The Columbus Monthly*.[13] Falla's keen interest in Columbus (his library contains dozens of books on the explorer written in the nineteenth and twentieth centuries) may be attributed to his grandmother's American ancestry. This interest manifested itself years later when Falla apotheosized Columbus in the cantata *Atlántida*, his unfinished magnum opus.

Like the other well-to-do children of Cadiz, Manuel was raised by a *nodriza* or nursemaid. La Morilla (the Moor),[14] as she was called, instilled in her charge an intimate knowledge of the song, the lore, and the superstition of Andalusia. The poet Lorca, who was very close to Falla during the years that they both lived in Granada (1919-23), has described the role of the nursemaid in the upbringing of an Andalusian child:

> The rich boy has a poor nursemaid who gives him her savage milk and infuses him with the essence of his people. These nurses, along with the cleaning women and other humble servants, have for a long time carried out the important task of transmitting ballads, songs, and stories to the houses of the aristocrats and the middle-class.[15]

Perhaps it was La Morilla who taught Falla his compassion for the poor, his suspicion of civil authority,[16] and his Andalusian superstitiousness about drafts, flies, and evil omens.[17]

Falla's youthful encounters with disease and death also left their mark on him. His grandfather Manuel, from whom he inherited his love for music and tobacco, died when he was eight years old. The following year (1885), a virulent strain of cholera swept Cadiz, claiming 554 victims, among them Falla's aunt Magdalena.[18] As a result of this incident, Falla developed a great fear of contagion, which he sought to combat with a severe daily regimen. Every morning he exercised, washed, and dressed himself with meticulous care. This ritual included a spiritual as well as

physical preparation (manifestations perhaps of his
staunch religious upbringing). Viniegra tells us that
the composer refused to speak to anyone before 1 P.M.
during his years in Paris (1907-14).[19] According to
Francisco García Lorca (the poet's brother), Falla spent
a full hour every morning brushing his teeth.[20] Falla
followed this schedule in Argentina (1939-46), but he
may well have adhered to the same or a similar routine
during his years in Granada (1920-39):

> Awaken at 9 A.M. Ritual of ablution, exercise,
>   and silence.
> Breakfast at noon followed by composition, study,
>   or correspondence.
> Dinner at 4 P.M. followed by a siesta.
> *Merienda* or "tea" at 7:30 P.M. followed by more
>   work.
> Supper at midnight.[21]

The specters of disease and death that had so impressed Falla during the Cadiz cholera epidemic of 1885
never ceased to haunt him. A week after his mother's
death (on 22 July 1919) he was terrified that he himself
might be exposed to some contagious disease in Granada,
where he and his sister sought repose:

> I would greatly appreciate any information about
> prices and the condition of inexpensive flats for
> two, near the Alhambra of course. Is there any
> typhus there?[22]

Falla's feelings for his father, like those of
Beethoven for his, were ambiguous, for both composers
far surpassed their fathers in accomplishment and, as
a result, found it difficult to respect them.[23] Although Don José received an inheritance of two million
pesetas (about $400,000) at the death of his father-in-
law in 1884,[24] he could not keep the family shipping
business afloat after 1900, and thus his son Manuel
became the family breadwinner at the age of twenty-four.
This responsibility was a godsend; overnight Falla was
transformed from a dreamy youth who played and composed
romantic piano pieces into a mature artist capable of

winning national competitions in piano performance and
opera composition.[25]

Falla left Cadiz in 1897 to enroll as a piano student at the National Conservatory in Madrid. His extra-
ordinary talent and ambition enabled him to complete
in just two years, the equivalent of three years of
solfege and seven years of piano study.[26] Until his
family joined him in Madrid in 1900, Falla lived with
his aunt Emilia and her husband, José Ledesma.[27] De-
spite his frantic pace of study, Falla found time to
launch his career as a professional pianist. In the
spring of 1898, and the autumns of 1899 and 1900, he
played recitals in his native Cadiz, charging three
pesetas (about 80 cents) for a box and one peseta for
a balcony seat.[28] The only Spanish works on these programs were his own, for Falla had yet to outgrow the
Romantic repertoire that he had been taught at home
and in the conservatory--Chopin, Grieg, Mendelssohn,
Schumann--even his own nocturnes, preludes, and waltzes
sounded more like Chopin than Albéniz.[29]

Although he earned a little concertizing and publishing (see the work list in Chapter II), Falla turned
to teaching piano as his principal source of income.
The only way to earn a living in Spain as a composer
was to write a successful *zarzuela*, the Spanish counter-
part (with obligatory dancing) of the French *opéra-
comique* and the German *Singspiele*. Of the five *zarzuelas* that Falla composed between 1900 and 1903, only
one--*El amor de Inés*--was performed, and it was anything
but a box-office success (see work list). After having
failed as a *zarzuela* composer, Falla sought the advice
of the composer-musicologist Felipe Pedrell (1841-1922),
who had taught musicians of international acclaim, such
as Isaac Albéniz (1860-1909) and Enrique Granados
(1867-1919). Falla explained the importance of
Pedrell's theories to his own way of thinking about
music in a tribute written twenty years after they met
in Madrid:

> Pedrell was a master in the highest sense of the
> word. His advice and work opened a secure road
> for the musicians of Spain, one that would lead
> them to the creation of a noble and profoundly

national art.... This genre [the *zarzuela*], a
mixture of the Spanish *tonadilla* and Italian opera,
was nothing more than an artistic product for national or even local consumption.... [Pedrell's]
theories were based on the axiom put forth by Padre
Antonio Eximeno in the 18th century: each nation
should build its musical-artistic system on the
foundation of its own traditional music.[30]

Although Pedrell was not, strictly speaking,
Falla's teacher (their relationship was similar to that
of Rimsky-Korsakov and Stravinsky), his advice and encouragement emboldened Falla to concentrate his efforts
on composition rather than piano performance. In November 1904, shortly after Pedrell moved to Barcelona,
Falla began composing *La vida breve* for a contest that
promised the composer of the best "one-act Spanish opera" 2500 pesetas and a performance of his work.[31]
Falla and his librettist Carlos Fernández Shaw took
first prize with their opera *La vida breve*, which would
have been performed had the Royal Academy of Fine Arts
found an impresario willing to finance the staging of
a work that was neither *zarzuela* nor Italian opera.[32]
Aware of his countrymen's predilection for Italian opera
and Spanish *zarzuela*, Falla resigned himself to taking
La vida breve to Paris. He was thirty-one years old
when he left Madrid, where for ten years he had strug-
gled to make a name for himself. Although he had won
some recognition, his association with Pedrell (whose
music was not well received) had a far greater impact
on Falla than any short-lived fame he might have enjoyed
as a composer of *zarzuelas*. By leaving the security
of his home and family (as he had in 1897), he again
thrust himself into a challenging musical environment.

The Paris Years (1907-1914)
The self-reliance that Falla had developed in
Madrid stood him in good stead in Paris, where foreign
composers were expected to ally themselves with a particular school. Unlike his contemporary Joaquín Turina,
who submitted himself to the rigors of the Schola Can-
torum, Falla maintained his independence, just as he
had in Madrid, by seeking the advice of musicians who

had made significant contributions (Dukas and Debussy)
and whose views were compatible with his own. Indeed
one might argue that he was excessively self-reliant in
refusing commissions (including one from Tito Ricordi,
which we shall discuss later) that would have furthered
his career and offered him important artistic chal-
lenges.[33]

It is said that Falla arrived at the Quai d'Orsay
with nothing more than a letter of introduction to the
pianist Ricardo Viñes, who was then living in Paris.[34]
Given the following sequence of events, it is possible
to narrow his date of arrival to mid-July. Beginning
in January of 1906, Joaquín Turina wrote Falla frequently in an effort to convince him to come join him
in Paris. The last of Turina's letters addressed to
the Falla family apartment on calle Serrano 70, in Madrid, is dated 21 June 1907.[35] The first of Falla's
letters addressed in Paris is dated 16 August 1907.[36]
In an attempt to save time, he wrote his family and his
librettist nearly identical letters although the one
to Fernández Shaw does include some important chronological data: he writes that he received the letter from
Fernández Shaw dated the tenth, the day after he arrived
in Paris, but that he had not written because he left
Paris a few days later on a tour of France, Belgium,
Germany, and Switzerland.

According to these parallel accounts of his first
month outside of Spain, Falla was the conductor-
accompanist for a small theater troupe that was performing a pantomime by André Wormser (1851-1926), *L'enfant
prodigue*. Several of Falla's biographers would have
us believe that he suffered great hardships while leading the romantic life of a bohemian musician. Campoamor
González contends that "Falla accepted this job with
resignation, thereby initiating himself into the bohemian and picturesque life of the itinerant musician."[37]
Demarquez compounds Falla's suffering by calling this
tour a financial disaster.[38] Falla himself provides
us with a more realistic account:

> I am in good health, thank God, for the trip
> suited me well. I am also in much better spirits
> than a month ago. You asked for press clippings

which I cannot send because I have not seen any.
My work was limited to *L'enfant prodigue*, a tre-
mendous success. I was unable to perform concert
works because the pianos were so bad and because
I had no time to practice: we traveled at a cine-
matographic pace. In Martigny there was no orchestra for the Overture, so I played it alone
on the piano. It was such a success that they
continued to applaud long after I had finished.[39]

In his letter to Fernández Shaw, Falla spoke more of
their opera than of his recent tour:

When I arrived in Paris my agent told me that
[Mr. P. Ganet] could translate *La vida breve* and
produce it here as well, since Paris has four opera houses....
    Regarding the artistic merits of this gentle-
man, I know only what my agent has told me. He
has produced works in Paris and is now translating
a dramatic adaptation of Balzac's *La cousine belle*
for Barcelona and Madrid....
    Have you spoken to the management of the
Teatro Real about *La vida breve*? Before leaving
Madrid I was told by members of the Music Section
of the Royal Academy that the matter would be considered in October.... Let's hope that it will
be performed in the coming season. Believe me
when I say that my enthusiasm has not diminished,
for I grow fonder of our opera every day. I
brought it to Paris so that I could revise it once
more before showing it to anyone. I shall make
no more than a few minute changes.[40]

It appears that the first eminent Parisian who
heard *La vida breve* was Paul Dukas. Falla's biographer
Pahissa has conjured up a dramatic vision of the initial
meeting between the Frenchman and Spaniard: upon hearing
Falla's rendering of the opera, Dukas is purported to
have said, "we shall have it performed at the Opéra-
Comique."[41] Indeed the opera was eventually staged
there--seven years after this meeting--but it is doubt-
ful that Dukas was in any way responsible for this.

By his own account, Falla solicited advice rather than
assistance:

> I won my first major victory shortly after my ar-
> rival in Paris, when I visited Dukas (Debussy was
> out of town). In that first meeting I told Dukas
> that I had come to Paris to study the techniques
> of the modern French school to see if I could in-
> corporate any of these into my own way of feeling
> music. He asked me to play something that would
> give him an idea of what I was doing; I played *La
> vida breve*, and never shall I forget the generous
> interest with which he listened....
>   Next year the most important part of my plans
> --the staging of *La vida breve*, in whatever theatre
> --should, God willing, come to pass.[42]

Falla's artistic mission in Paris was to an extent
hampered by practical concerns: in his first letter to
his parents, Falla described upcoming obligations--
another tour with a pantomime troupe beginning on 21
August, and a recital tour with a talented singer in
October. The August-September stint he considered
"nothing more than a stepping stone to more important
things,"[43] but he looked forward to the October tour,
which in addition to offering him a greater artistic
challenge, promised to be a more lucrative venture: "I
expect to earn 1500 francs or more...."[44] Falla's
seven-year struggle to obtain a performance of *La vida
breve* was made all the more difficult by this constant
search for new sources of income. After returning from
this third tour he once again faced impresarios' refus-
als of *La vida breve* and a desperate pecuniary situation
as well:

> I think you'll agree that it would be prudent to
> accept the offer of the [Teatro] Real's impre-
> sarios for a premiere coinciding with or following
> its foreign premiere....
>   I want your opinion on a new idea of mine.
> I would like to write, for pay, a musical column
> for one of Madrid's newspapers, like the one
> Joaquín Nin (who also lives here) writes for the

newspapers of Barcelona. I believe that it would
be of real artistic interest, given that Paris is
one of the principal musical centers of Europe,
as you well know. Although I am new to this, I
could easily consult with competent people regarding its literary form.[45]

Nothing became of this scheme; however, Falla did later
contribute to *La revue musicale* and to various Spanish
periodicals.

Falla's preoccupation with money diminished, once
he had found Parisian publishers interested in his
short, characteristic pieces for voice and for piano
solo. Debussy and Dukas introduced him to Durand, who
published his Four Spanish Pieces.[46] He performed them
at his Paris debut in a concert of the Société Nationale
de Musique on 27 March 1909. His second Paris premiere
took place on 4 May 1910, when his *Trois melodies* on
poems of Théophile Gautier were sung.[47] Falla dedicated
the third of these songs, "Séguidille," to Madame
Debussy, a token no doubt, of his appreciation for her
sympathy and her husband's help. Debussy and Dukas
both facilitated Falla's entrance into the rather closed
musical circle of Paris. Dukas, for instance, introduced him to his own countryman, Isaac Albéniz, who in
turn introduced Falla to the future translator of *La
vida breve*, Paul Milliet.[48] Milliet, a member of the
board of directors of the National Society of Authors,
saw to the opera's publication, once he had translated
it into French.[49]

Certain scenes from Falla's early days in Paris
have been grotesquely distorted by Pahissa, a Spanish
composer living in exile in Argentina at the time that
he wrote his biography. In one such scene, Falla is
surrounded by Debussy, Dukas, Albéniz, and Ravel, when
he announces that Durand gave him only 300 francs for
his Four Spanish Pieces. To Falla's amazement, these
composers explain how they have literally given their
works away.[50] Pahissa exercises even greater poetic
license when he attributes the following declarations
to Falla:

Without Paris I would have remained neglected

> and forgotten, eking out an existence in Madrid
> as a piano teacher: the prize for my opera hung
> on the wall of our home and its score buried in a
> trunk....
>
> Publishing in Spain is worse than not pub-
> lishing at all. One might as well throw the music
> into a well.[51]

Although Falla would never have consented to the publication of these statements,[52] I have translated them
here because they raise important questions regarding
his attitudes toward Spain and Paris. Unfortunately,
Pahissa's statements are all-too-often cited as fact.[53]
Falla himself addressed this question in an article
published fifteen years after he had returned to live
in Spain:

> No one in Spain wants to admit that music is an
> expensive art form, an indispensable luxury that
> brings honor to this nation, which has proven its
> musical worth to the whole world. For that reason,
> not only is official support urgently needed, but
> also that of private organizations....
>
> Due to these unfavorable circumstances, our
> musical rebirth has been facilitated. This might
> seem absurd, but had it not been for the invinci-
> ble difficulties that our composers encountered
> in Spain, they would not have chosen expatriation
> as a last hope. This expatriation in turn put
> them in direct contact with the music of Europe,
> whose universal significance provided a model for
> our own music. They worked with enthusiasm and
> faith, making stimulating acquaintances and cordial
> friendships. Eventually their works were published
> and performed: this experimental field of battle
> was one more critical step in their artistic de-
> velopment.[54]

Falla's description of the situation that the Spanish
composers of his generation faced is strongly colored
by his own experiences, for several of his contempo-
raries—Turina, for example—were much more successful
in Spain (and less successful in Paris) than he.

Although many of Falla's biographers make him out
to be an ardent nationalist,[55] we must bear in mind
that most of these writers were subjected to the oppres-
sive censorship of Generalísimo Franco (1939-75).
Nevertheless, it seems that even those who have not
portrayed him as a flag-waving patriot have tried to
fit Falla into some sort of mold. Ramón Pérez de
Ayala[56] makes him out to be a monk; Luis Jiménez,[57] a
psychoneurotic; and Viniegra,[58] a provincial homebody.

While it is true that the family of his uncle,
Pedro Javier Matheu, was living in Paris when Falla
arrived, they moved to Spain early in 1909. Furthermore, he never lived with the Matheus or relied on them
for any financial help. Falla's letters to his immedi-
ate family indicate that he wanted to be looked upon
as a provider rather than a dependent of his family:

> I did not want to let another day pass before I
> wrote. I have only a minute, however, for I am
> swamped with obligations. I needn't tell you how
> much I enjoyed your greetings for the new year,
> nor how much I hope that you, Mother, had the best
> of days....
> Regarding [*Nights in the*] *Gardens* [*of Spain*],
> send it any way you can, by rail or whatever.
> Pedro [Matheu] cannot bring it for the simple
> reason that he is moving there; he has already
> sold his furniture to Turina and is transferring
> his rental contract to him as well.
> Here we do not have the cold and wind that
> is making you so ill, Father. Go to the store of
> the Society [of Spanish Authors] and withdraw my
> trimestral [royalties]. While you are there, ask
> them to send me three copies of "Tus ojillos
> negros." Tell them that they are needed for con-
> certs in Paris and Bordeaux, where the song is in
> great demand. The Four Spanish Pieces have been
> published. In a few days I shall send you a copy
> and also what I can spare for this month.[59]

Falla rarely traveled to Spain during these years,
and when he did it was for professional as well as personal reasons. During the Christmas holidays of 1907,

for example, he returned to give a series of piano recitals.[60] After changing his residence three times in
Paris, he settled, in November 1908,[61] at the Hôtel
Kleber, 7 rue de Bellow, XVIe (not avenue Kleber as
Pahissa states) where he resided for the rest of his
stay in Paris. Given this relative stability one won-
ders if Debussy did in fact say that "Falla moves as
frequently as Beethoven did."[62]
        More often than not when Falla left Paris it was
to play his opera *La vida breve* for some theater director. In the autumn of 1911 he traveled to Brussels,
where he almost succeeded in convincing Messrs.
Kufferath and Guide of the Théâtre de la Monet to accept
his opera.[63] This trip was preceded by one to London,
where in addition to showing theater directors his opera, Falla accompanied a singer in a concert at Aeolian
Hall on 24 May 1911.[64] Numerous accounts relate Falla's
experiences in Milan, which he purportedly visited at
the invitation of the publisher Tito Ricordi. In 1911,
Puccini allegedly turned down a libretto by Adami based
on the play *Genio alegre* by the Spanish playwrights
Joaquín and Serafín Quíntero. This libretto was subsequently offered to Falla, who, to Tito Ricordi's
amazement, turned it down as well.[65]
        After rejections from theaters in Madrid, London,
Brussels, Milan, and Paris,[66] the acceptance of *La vida
breve* by the management of the Casino municipal at Nice
seemed a miracle. Its premiere (on 1 April 1913) was
a resounding success, as were the many performances
that followed at the Opéra-Comique of Paris during
January, February, and March of 1914.[67]
        Falla showed no indication of wanting to return
to Spain after his "primary objective" for coming to
Paris had been accomplished. Even the menace of war
was insufficient to stir him:

        Everyone here speaks of nothing but the possibility
        of war. We shall see what will become of this.
        I cannot believe there will be a war, because God
        would not permit such a horrible thing to occur:
        all of Europe and even the whole world would
        suffer.[68]

Three days after Falla wrote this letter, Germany declared war on France. Falla described the food shortage
in Paris to Turina in a letter written that very day,
and in spite of the risk of remaining there, he did so
for at least another eight days.[69]
     Falla had grown so accustomed to his independence
in Paris, that when he finally left, he chose to travel
with the theater company of his friends the Martínez
Sierras rather than return to his family home in Madrid.[70] When he did stop in Madrid to assist in the
staging of his opera he was met with open arms:

> Now that Falla has returned to his homeland, we
> have yet another valiant hero to fight for the re-
> birth of Spanish music.[71]

Although he prized his triumphs abroad, Falla was over-
joyed to find his music accepted in Spain, where he
hoped to see the *zarzuela* eclipsed by Spanish opera and
concert music.[72]
     Several years after his return to Spain, Falla
laid down guidelines for the "modern (Spanish) composer"
in an article entitled "Our Music":

> One must draw one's inspiration, as much as is
> possible, from the people. He who attempts to
> base his music on particular folk melodies, how-
> ever, will succeed only in creating a caricature
> of what he had set out to accomplish.[73]

In this and other articles Falla named those that he
believed had contributed to the rebirth of Spanish music. In addition to Albéniz, Granados, and Turina--all
of whom had lived in Paris--Falla singled out Debussy
and Ravel for distinction. His article in *La revue
musicale* entitled "Claude Debussy et Espagne" begins
with the provocative claim that "Claude Debussy wrote
Spanish music without ever having gone to Spain."[74]
Falla found even more to admire in the music, and per-
son, of Maurice Ravel, a quiet and self-contained man
like himself. In his discourse on Ravel's musical background, Falla inadvertantly blurs the distinction between his own heritage and that of Ravel:

How can I explain the subtle Spanish qualities of
our musician when he himself has said that his
only contact with Spain was having been born near
its border? The answer is simple: Ravel's Spain
was an ideal conception transmitted to him through
his mother. I derived great pleasure from hearing
this woman recount, in her exquisitely clear Spanish, the days of her youth in Madrid. Although
the epoch she described preceded my own, vestiges
of it were still apparent in the customs of my
family. I could therefore understand the fascina-
tion with which her son (from the days of his infancy) must have received these melancholy recollections, enlivened, no doubt, by evocative melodies of the sort that he himself later created.[75]

It is natural then that Falla should have felt more at
home in prewar Paris dreaming about an idealized Spain
with his friends, than in Spain, where traditional music
and dance had been subsumed by the *zarzuela*, "an artistic product for national ... consumption."[76] The dates
of Ravel's and Debussy's Spanish compositions are well
worth noting for they coincide with Falla's stay in
Paris: *Rapsodie espagnole* (1907), *L'heure espagnol*
(1910), and "Iberia" from the *Images* for orchestra
(1909).

The Three-Cornered Hat (1916-19)

Once Falla had established himself as a composer
of orchestral music with *La vida breve* and *Nights in
the Gardens of Spain*, he abandoned the popular genres
of the salon (songs, characteristic piano pieces, etc.)
in order to compose for the theater and concert hall.
One can see the evolution of Falla's orchestration in
the lavish *Nights in the Gardens of Spain*, which was
originally composed for piano solo. Although the original piano version is not extant, it seems that the
work was begun in Madrid, transformed into a set of
"symphonic impressions" in Paris, and completed in Spain
during the year (1914-15) that Falla was touring Spain
with the Martínez Sierras.[77] The impressionistic flavor
of *Nights in the Gardens of Spain* suggests that he intended it as a tribute to (in his own words) "the

techniques of the modern French school."[78]   The accounts
of Demarquez and Crichton[79] are misguided, for the prem-
ise of their argument that *Nights* is strictly a Paris
work is false: its dates could not have been 1911-15,
because Falla asked his parents to send its drafts to
him from Spain, which he had left in July 1907.[80]

At the same time that Falla was perfecting the
works for which he is best remembered, *Nights in the
Gardens of Spain* and *The Three-Cornered Hat*, he was
also composing incidental music for the theater of
Gregorio Martínez Sierra.[81]   Among the plays, translations of plays, and pantomimes by Martínez Sierra for
which Falla provided music are *Amanecer* (1914), *El
amor brujo* (original version, 1914), *Othello* (1915),
La pasión (1915), and *El corregidor y la molinera*
(1916).[82]   Although he may have derived great satisfaction from composing music for the moment, Falla later
destroyed the scores and parts of these frivolous
pieces.   The little incidental music that has survived
does not owe its existence to chance, for Falla was a
meticulous collector of anything he considered valuable,
including his complete correspondence (letters he received and copies of all that he sent), musical
sketches, etc.   Like Dukas, who destroyed much of what
he composed,[83] Falla was severely self-critical and
would publish a composition only after he had spent
years perfecting it.

The music for two of these theatrical productions
has survived in a substantially revised form: the ballet
scores for *The Three-Cornered Hat* (1919) and *El amor
brujo* (1925).   The inspiration for the first of these
ballets was provided by Serge Diaghilev, who brought
his company of Russian dancers to Spain (a neutral coun-
try) during the First World War.   Until now all we have
been told about the pantomime entitled *El corregidor y
la molinera* is that it was first performed on 7 April
1917, and later transformed into *The Three-Cornered
Hat*, which received its premiere in London on 22 July
1919.[84]

The recent discovery of an autograph (unorches-
trated) draft of *El corregidor y la molinera* has made
a comparison of the original pantomime and the published

ballet possible.[85]   Other important sources for the
history of the pantomime's adaptation are contemporary
newspaper accounts[86] and the memoirs of members of the
Ballets Russes, especially those of Leonide Massine
who choreographed the ballet.

The first of the works' two parts are nearly the
same, but Part 2 of the ballet builds steadily to a
climax while Part 2 of the pantomime has neither the
dramatic nor musical resources to do so.   Falla himself
has described the shape of the ballet:

> ... the size of the ensemble in Part 1 of the bal-
> let has been intentionally limited to that of a
> chamber orchestra.   Later, on the contrary, from
> the beginning of Part 2, the choreographic and
> orchestral elements gradually increase, culminating
> in the Final Dance.[87]

In this Final Dance, Falla and Massine transcend the
limitations of conventional theater by utilizing the
full orchestra and full corps of dancers to enact the
central allegory of the ballet: the victory of the people, led by the clever miller, over ineffectual monar-
chical authority, depicted by the foolish old governor
or *corregidor*.   The *pantomime* ends with a brief (twenty-
measure) Finale, which is musically and dramatically
weak: the curtain falls on a farcical tussle between
the half-dozen characters.   The *ballet*'s Final Dance
is a substantial rondo-form number (361 measures); its
musical climax, the final refrain, coincides with the
dramatic high point of the entire ballet--the tossing
of the *corregidor* in a blanket--a powerful image bor-
rowed from Goya's painting, "El pelele."

Falla's collaboration with the cosmopolitan members
of the Ballets Russes made him aware of the infinite
possibilities of the modern stage.   His experience in
composing for the theater had previously been limited
by the provinciality of his librettists Fernández Shaw
and Martínez Sierra.   Indeed it is conceivable that
this lack of sophistication was an important factor in
the rejection of *La vida breve* by so many theaters.
El corregidor y la molinera's scenario[88] is full of
silly gestures, earthy expressions, and regionalisms,

and is lacking the social significance of the novel on
which it is based.[89]   The characters of the ballet, on
the other hand, are equivalent to those of the original
story: the miller (common folk) and the *corregidor* (ar-
istocracy) vie for the love of the miller's wife
(Spain).   A comparison of corresponding scenes from the
pantomime and ballet illuminates the extent to which
they differ.

Part 2 of the pantomime and ballet open with the
Neighbor's Dance (the only dance in the pantomime),
which sets the time of action as night (Part 1 was set
in broad daylight).   In the pantomime this dance is
followed by the ridiculous Seduction Scene in which
the miller tries to coax his coy wife to come to bed.
In the ballet this scene is replaced by the Miller's
Dance in which a handsome young miller (as opposed to
the pantomime's humpback) displays his virility by dancing the most difficult of flamenco dances, the *farruca*.

Surely Pahissa is mistaken in his claim that the
music for the Miller's Dance was composed in twenty-four
hours, at the behest of Diaghilev.[90]   According to
Massine, who choreographed and danced its premiere,
this *farruca* and the *jota* (Final Dance) were begun in
the summer of 1917, when he and Falla traveled together
in Andalusia.[91]   The following summer Diaghilev hired
an exceptionally talented Spaniard named Félix Fernández
García to dance in his corps de ballet and to teach
Massine the *farruca*.[92]   Félix, known as "el loco," had
great expectations when he joined the Ballets Russes.
His lack of discipline, however, made him unsuitable
for the corps de ballet, much less the role of the
miller to which he aspired.   His career, like that of
the great Nijinsky, ended in insanity: when he learned
that Massine would be dancing the *farruca* in the London
Three-Cornered Hat rather than himself, Félix broke
into the Church of St. Martin-in-the-Fields and madly
danced his *farruca* there.[93]

After having collaborated with outstanding talents
like Diaghilev, Massine, and Picasso (who designed the
ballet's sets and costumes),[94] Falla had no reason to
return to composing incidental music for Martínez
Sierra's provincial entertainments, for he now knew
enough to prepare his own scenarios and librettos.   This

he did in the dramatic works that followed his ballets:
El retablo de Maese Pedro (1923) and Atlántida (1926–
46, unfinished). The ingenuity of El retablo's scenario
--a puppet play within a puppet play--evidences the
great strides he had made since the Ballets Russes arrived in Spain in 1916.

Falla, however, felt ill at ease in the vulnerable
position into which The Three-Cornered Hat (the Ballets
Russes' most successful postwar oeuvre) had put him.
Like Stravinsky, whom Diaghilev browbeat over the size
of royalties for The Firebird and Petrushka,[95] Falla
was subjected to this director's notorious haggling:

> On Saturday I saw Diaghilev in his hotel. It is
> impossible to argue with him,...
>
> Diaghilev is paying, but at an exasperating rate
> ... so far I've received 750 pesetas [about $150].
> ... I'm exhausted from this economic battle with
> the Muscovite theater.[96]

Ultimately Falla even made artistic concessions to the
iron-willed Diaghilev, who after the London premiere
cut a substantial number (the Corregidor's Dance) from
the production that his company was taking to Paris,
Rome, Monte Carlo, etc. For two years Falla tolerated
this situation, but in April 1922 he complained to his
publisher that

> ... the orchestra parts for The Three-Cornered
> Hat redone by Diaghilev must be destroyed: they
> are unplayable because of the cuts they contain
> and because they are poor copies.[97]

The publisher, to whom Diaghilev still owed money for
the London premiere, gladly passed this complaint on
to him. Diaghilev responded with a calculated threat
to Falla:

> Certainly you want to see the same artists perform
> your lovely work again with the same mise-en-scéne
> of Picasso's, of which, I believe, you are quite
> fond. Unless it is staged, it seems inevitable

to me that it will die in the archives.[98]

Unlike Stravinsky, who was willing to fight Diaghilev on his own terms, Falla was a gentle, self-effacing man who shunned violence.

After the excitement of the London and Paris premieres of his ballet, Falla retired to the sleepy town of Granada, where he lived with his sister from 1920 until 1939. It was quite natural for María del Carmen to take her mother's place as Manuel's companion, for he had grown up surrounded by women--his mother, his nursemaid, his sister, aunt, and grandmother. In Paris, Madame Debussy, Madame Adiny-Milliet (his translator's wife), and other ladies (many of whom had works dedicated to them) fussed over this delicate soul.

Another factor that contributed to Falla's withdrawal from society was the death of both his parents in 1919. By a cruel twist of fate his mother died on 22 July, the date of *The Three-Cornered Hat*'s premiere; it is staggering to think of the effect that this coincidence must have had on a man as superstitious as Falla. He left London immediately upon hearing of her illness but learned of her death en route to Madrid. When he arrived

> He could not bring himself to enter [his home], and remained in the vestibule, completely disheartened. Sitting on a chair, without uttering a single word, he burst into tears like a child. Never had I seen him cry, so I was incredulous, thinking him too strong for tears.[98]

Falla had been considerably less affected by the death of his father some months earlier; in response to a letter of sympathy from the painter Ignacio Zuloaga, Falla wrote:

> I truly appreciate your condolences for my great misfortune. I too send you mine for [the poor health] you have suffered. I shall visit you when you return from Seville. How much I'd like to chat![100]

A few days later Falla returned to work, and in less
than two months, he had finished copying the parts and
score for the Spanish concert performance of *The Three-
Cornered Hat* (17 June 1919) that preceded its London
premiere.[101]

After the death of his mother, Falla underwent a
crisis of conscience that affected his work as well as
his way of life. Suddenly he felt remorse at having
devoted his efforts to theatrical works whose subjects
were erotic love, sorcery, and deceit. In 1923, for
example, Falla crossed out the following incantation,

> (Religiously) Incense holy! Incense new!
>   Out with the evil and in with the
>   good![102]

which sets the scenario for his "Danza del fin del día"
(later the "Ritual Fire Dance") from the original version of *El amor brujo* (1915). A more significant dem-
onstration of this new moral vigilance was his decision
to leave the opera *Fuego Fatuo* (which he had begun a
year before his mother's death) incomplete. Although
little is known about this work's history, its librettist María Martínez Sierra explains that Falla refused
to complete the score because he found its subject--
the struggle between a young man and two women (the
archetypal good woman and evil woman)--morally objec-
tionable.[103]

Falla's return to Andalusia, the region of his
birth, and to his sister, the last of his family (his
brother Germán had gone to New York), did not stifle
his creative drive; on the contrary, the peace and security that he found in Granada fostered a new burst
of energy. Although far removed from the world of impresarios and high society, Falla was not artistically
isolated, since he associated with the talented young
writers (including the poet Lorca) who lived in Granada.
This "Generation of 1927" that championed the poets
and dramatists of Spain's Golden Age--Falla contributed
to their tercentenary homage to Góngora (d. 1627)--
doubtless influenced his decision to write a puppet
play based on the *Quijote* of Cervantes, a contemporary
of Góngora. Indeed, Lorca, Picasso, Falla, and several

other Spaniards were on the cutting edge of the neoclassical movement that swept Western Europe during
the 1920's. *El retablo de Maese Pedro* (1923) and the
Harpsichord Concerto (1926) are both in a neoclassical
style and both contributed immensely to the revival of
the harpsichord by incorporating that instrument in a
modern musical idiom. Falla, who was the first composer in the 20th century to write for harpsichord,
was a good friend of Wanda Landowska, to whom his Concerto is dedicated.[104]

    Characteristics of Falla's neo-classic style are
evident in *The Three-Cornered Hat*, a watershed in his
career. In the process of working with Massine,
Picasso, and the other artists in Diaghilev's retinue,
he developed the skills and independence that he needed
in order to work alone.[105]

The Second Republic (1931-36)

    To understand the creative crisis that Falla under-
went during this period of his life, one must acknowledge the effect that Spain's political upheaval had on
him.[106] From 1902 until 1923, King Alfonso XIII reigned
as constitutional monarch of a semi-feudal Spain. During this period, he and his ministers fought to keep
the status quo, opposing the concepts of modern government—free trade, industrialization, and social reform—
that the other nations of Western Europe were gradually
adopting. Geographically isolated from the rest of
Europe by a great wall of mountains, Spain separated
herself politically and economically as well by levying
high tariffs and by remaining neutral in the First World
War.

    In 1923 the delicate balance that Alfonso had tried
to maintain between the parliament and the military
was upset, and a protest against the military by Catalan
separatists and university students served as an excuse
for General Miguel Primo de Rivera to stage a coup
d'état. The transition from a constitutional government
to a dictatorship made little difference to most Spaniards; indeed the king himself accepted this benevolent
dictator, calling him "my Mussolini." For seven years
this pragmatic dictatorship maintained Spain's central
institutions—Nation, Church, and King—ignoring the

objections of students and Catalans who sought social
reform, regional autonomy, and individual rights. Although these opponents had little influence on the general public, by 1929 Primo's position was considerably
weakened by runaway inflation.

Spain's economic woes and the alienation of her
generals ultimately brought an end to the dictatorship.
In the brief hiatus, September 1930 to April 1931, between Primo de Rivera's fall from power and the Republican revival, King Alfonso tried desperately to gain
favor with his subjects, but his opponents, who now
included Socialists and Communists, made a return to
constitutional monarchy impossible. On 14 April 1931,
the king left Spain after learning that the Socialist-
Republican bloc had won a majority of the municipal
elections held in the provincial capitals. A Revolu-
tionary Committee declared the Second Republic that
same day, and for the next six years, Spain joined the
European race to industrialize, to reform--in short--
to progress. Although Falla professed to have no interest in politics, the politics of Spain did indeed have
a great effect on his work. The stormy years of the
Republic proved as disruptive to Falla's work as the
torpid years of the dictatorship had been favorable.

As Primo rose to power in 1923, Falla was living
a quiet life in his small house beneath the enchanted
walls of the Alhambra. There, far removed from the
political intrigue and noise of Madrid and Paris, he
composed his most sublime works, *El retablo de Maese
Pedro* (1926) and the Harpsichord Concerto (1926). Although he made an occasional trip to Paris--*El retablo*,
commissioned by the Princess de Polignac, received its
premiere there--Falla spent less than three weeks a
year, on the average, outside of Spain between 1920 and
1926. After he completed the Concerto, he was more
inclined to accept invitations to conduct and perform
his works,[107] in part, because he felt obliged to represent Spain in the International Society for Contemporary Music (ISCM).

Notwithstanding this purposeful renewal of social
activity, Falla remained first and foremost a composer;
no sooner had he completed his Concerto than he began
looking for a Spanish poem to set to music. In June

1926, on his return from an ISCM Festival in Zurich, he read an excerpt of the epic *L'Atlàntida* by the Catalan priest Jacint Verdaguer (1845-1902).[108] This epic narration of Spain's birth from the ruins of Atlantis greatly impressed Falla, who saw in Verdaguer's amalgam of biblical, mythological, and historical imagery the makings for a profound musical drama.

Upon his arrival in Granada, Falla immediately procured a copy of Verdaguer's *L'Atlàntida* and a Catalan grammar, for although he already knew some Catalan from his days with the Martínez Sierras in Barcelona, he wanted to be fluent in the language before attempting to adapt the libretto for his work. From 1926 until his death in 1946 Falla labored patiently on *Atlántida*, a work that in its final stages comprised three parts and a prologue, for orchestra, chorus, soloists, and mimed action (he usually referred to it as a scenic cantata). Although the history of Falla's struggle to complete *Atlántida* lies outside of the scope of this essay,[109] we shall briefly examine his compositional activity (which converged on *Atlántida*) during the Second Republic, a period in which he lost much of his creative drive.

Falla frequently attributed his slow rate of progress on *Atlántida* to problems with his health. Indeed he had suffered poor health since childhood, and later, in Paris and Madrid, he frequently wrote that he was unable to compose because of a cold or the flu. In 1928, however, an incipient tubercular infection (tuberculosis was quite common in Spain at that time) manifested itself in the form of iritis, inflammation of the iris. Several times during the last eighteen years of his life, Falla was incapacitated by attacks of iritis that prevented him from reading and writing.[110] This tuberculosis subsequently manifested itself in a variety of forms--hemorrhaging (with its accompanying dizzy spells), shortness of breath, and bone ailments-- all of which necessitated surgical intervention.[111] But in spite of the physical suffering to which he was condemned, he might have overcome this obstacle and completed *Atlántida* had his inner peace not been shattered by the noise, the secularism, and the senseless brutality that characterized this era of revolution (1931-36) and war (1936-39).

Falla did not, in principle, object to the Republic; indeed he welcomed most of the social reforms promised by republican leaders. He was concerned, however,
that violent acts would accompany an overly rapid change
in the social order:

> The manner in which this revolution has been car-
> ried out is miraculous. God willing, it will con-
> tinue to pursue a peaceful course.[112]

Falla was one of the many Spanish intellectuals and
artists who voiced their concern for Spain's future.
A declaration made by the philosopher Ortega y Gasset,
for example, gives us an idea of the volatility of this
transition: "After 14 April we shall all be something
other than we were."[113] Devout Catholics like Falla
were especially worried because many republicans were
intent upon avenging the Church's complicity with the
king and his dictator. These fears were well-founded;
the Republic was less than a month old when a minor
scuffle between a group of monarchists and republicans
touched off a series of church burnings in Madrid which
Spain's provisional government passively tolerated.
This attitude was in keeping with the government's new
anticlerical, if not anti-Catholic stance: Article 26
of the new constitution legislated the expulsion of
the Jesuits, the secularization of public education,
and--to the amazement of all--the separation of Church
and State. The ferocity with which this attack on the
Church was carried out transformed Falla into a dis-
illusioned and broken man: "The recent incidents, about
which you have doubtless read, have made these days the
most bitter of my life."[114]

Ironically, several of his closest companions were
socialists, agnostics, and/or liberals. Fernando de
los Ríos, Lorca's mentor and a friend of Falla, was
the Republic's first Minister of Justice. In several
letters to Ríos, Falla clarified his rather unusual
position on politics and the Church; for Falla was a
poor liberal (he gave most of his earnings to charity),
while most practicing Catholics in Spain were wealthy
conservatives who vehemently opposed the Republic's
policies of social reform. Although Falla claimed to

be apolitical, his views on every issue except the
Church coincided with those of his liberal friends:

> You are well-acquainted with my ideals, which tran-
> scend superficial political issues. I shall en-
> deavor, with all the strength of my soul, to care
> for the needs of the poor and to rectify the in-
> justices that they must bear.[115]

In June 1932, Falla denounced his government's attacks
on the Church by refusing an homage offered him by the
city of Seville: "If God is 'officially' denied any
sort of tribute, then how can I, his poor creature,
accept [this homage]."[116]

It is clear from circumstantial evidence, as well
as from his own testimony, that the state of Falla's
health frequently reflected that of his spirit. Attacks
against the Church ("collective blasphemy" in Falla's
words) in particular had devastating consequences. A
rash of church burnings in his native Cadiz, for example, was the cause of his severe relapse shortly before the outbreak of the Civil War.[117]

Given such a scenario of mental and physical suffering, it is not surprising that Falla made little
progress on *Atlántida* during the years of the Republic.
In order to see exactly how his work was affected, we
must go back to *Atlántida*'s beginnings.

Falla was intent upon keeping his *Atlántida* a se-
cret until he had a clear enough idea of its libretto
to convince Verdaguer's heirs to grant him permission
to proceed. It was two years after he began work on
this epic that Falla finally disclosed the contents of
his cantata to José María Sert, his proposed collaborator.[118] Even in this early conception of the work,
Falla emphasized the Christian elements of this story
of destruction and re-creation: the portrayal of Atlantis' demise as another Great Flood, of Hercules as an
instrument of divine retribution, and, most signifi-
cantly, of Columbus as "the dove, the bearer of Christ"
(*Colom Christoferens*). In this first version of the
cantata the sanctity of Columbus's mission is affirmed
by his sailors who sing hymns and litanies upon their
arrival in the New World. Falla ultimately fashioned

these sacred and devotional texts into the prayer-like
number "La salve en el mar" (included in the edition of
Atlántida completed by his student Ernesto Halffter).

Falla began composing the music for "La salve en
el mar" in February 1932, the same month in which he
wrote a will stipulating the most strictly moral performance of his works after his death.[119] He embarked
on the composition of this number with pious trepida-
tion; before he wrote a single note, he submitted its
text to the rector of a Jesuit college as a means of
self-imposed ecclesiastical censure.[120] The weight of
this moral responsibility in combination with the an-
guish that he had experienced over the church burnings
of May 1931 overwhelmed Falla, forcing him to abandon
his work after suffering "a severe attack of nerves":

> My brother Manuel has suffered an attack of nerves
> of the most severe sort, and the doctors have had
> him on a regimen of complete isolation ... the
> best plan seems for us to go to Palma [Mallorca],
> for we have not forgotten your generous invita-
> tion.... Since it will be only a brief visit, we
> want to stay in a pension: one that is clean and
> comfortable, but not luxurious, with plenty of
> sunlight and healthy food, and situated in a quiet
> neighborhood where there are neither gramaphones
> nor any other bothersome noises.[121]

What began as a "brief visit" turned into a lengthy
stay, because Falla's Mallorcan friend, Padre Juan María
Thomas, succeeded in finding him the pristine accommo-
dations he needed in order to work.[122] There Falla
isolated himself from the noise and violence that had
driven him out of Granada. After living in Mallorca
from February to June 1933, and from December 1933 to
June 1934, he returned to Granada with renewed hopes
for himself and for *Atlántida*, which he expected to
complete by the end of 1934;[123] however, problems arose
with the "Salve," which he worked on between February
and August 1935:[124] his doubts about the moral propriety
of its text re-surfaced and again he submitted it to
ecclesiastical censure as he had three years earlier.[125]
Not only were his particular fears about "La salve en

el mar" revived, but also those doubts about the recti-
tude of his entire ouevre: on 9 August 1935 he revised
his will to prohibit stagings of any of his works after
his death, unless his heirs be in dire need of royalties
that such stagings would earn.[126]

Clearly Falla had not lost his capacity to create,
for while he labored in vain on the "Salve," he composed
a moving "Pour le tombeau de Paul Dukas" to the memory
of his friend who had died in May 1935. Indeed he became so obsessed with the need to work for others that
he never allowed himself the satisfaction of finishing
his *Atlántida*, which by 1935 was two-thirds complete.
Since 1926, the year in which he gave us his last major
work, the Harpsichord Concerto, Falla had composed several short pieces, all homages to great artists.[127]
During the Civil War (1936-39) he sequestered himself
in Granada and dutifully worked on an orchestral suite,
each movement of which was based on an homage previously
composed for Debussy (1920), Dukas (1927), the conductor
Enrique Arbós (1934), and Felipe Pedrell (1935). This
vicious war, which claimed the lives of many of Falla's
friends, was finally brought to an end when Franco's
Nationalists (with the assistance of Italy and Germany)
ousted Spain's legitimate government. Falla and his
sister left Granada for Argentina, where they lived
until his death in 1946.

Like other exiled artists who had made their homes
in Latin America, Falla was welcomed with open arms.
The success that his suite *Homenajes* enjoyed at its
premiere in Buenos Aires in November 1939 might have
rejuvenated Falla had his memories of the Civil War
and the prospects of world war not weighed so heavily
upon him. Although he led an active life in Argentina
--conducting benefit concerts, adapting works of Pedrell
and Luis de Victoria, and so on--Falla ultimately ques-
tioned the value of his profession or "trade" (*oficio*)
as he called it.

Perhaps Falla's last musical contributions were
his least significant, but his love for his fellow man
was never stronger than it was in his final years. Until his death on 23 November 1946, Falla lived an aus-
tere existence, giving all he could spare to charities,
including the refugee camps in Southern France that

housed thousands of exiled Republicans. For although
the brutalities of this world had destroyed his will
to compose, Falla found true contentment in foregoing
the pleasures of the body for those of the spirit. As
an epilogue, I quote from one of Falla's last letters,
a letter to the woman he would have liked to have mar-
ried:

> It seems as though the earth were being enveloped
> by a vast mystery, causing us to wonder if we are
> at the end of the second (postdiluvian) generation
> of man.... I must confess that as I work, I often
> ask myself whether my time would be better spent
> doing something else ... something more spiri-
> tual.[128]

Notes

1. Darius Milhaud to Paul Claudel, December 1929, quoted in Paul Claudel, *Correspondance Paul Claudel-Darius Milhaud*, Cahiers Paul Claudel no. 3 (Paris: Gallimard, 1962), p. 109.

2. I would like to take this opportunity to express my appreciation to María Isabel de Falla, the composer's niece and sole heir, who granted me free access to her uncle's papers. All materials quoted here are from that collection unless otherwise noted, and all translations are my own.

3. By the Genoese artist, Nicolai Barabino. See Antonio Campoamor González, *Manuel de Falla, 1876-1946* (Madrid: Sedmay Ediciones, 1976), p. 23.

4. With Carmen and Carlos Martel Viniegra, *Vida íntima de Manuel de Falla* (Cadiz: Excma. Diputacion, 1966), p. 34.

5. Ibid., p. 31.

6. *Falla: biografía ilustrada* (Barcelona: Ediciones Destino, 1968), p. 8.

7. *Vida íntima*, p. 36f. Although he has provided us with this useful facsimile, he failed to read it carefully himself and made the egregious contention (on p. 35) that Falla was born on 20 November and baptized on 23 November.

8. Probably after Clemente Parodi, his future piano teacher, whose relationship to Falla's maternal grandfather, Manuel Parodi, has yet to be determined.

9. Viniegra, *Vida íntima*, p. 36.

10. *Falla 1876-1946*, pp. 217 ff.

11. Orozco, *Biografía*, pp. 10, 15.

12. E.g., *La ilustración artística, La ilustración ibérica, La hormiga de oro*, and the Parisian *Journal des demoiselles.* (Ibid., p. 10.)

13. *El cascabel, El burlón*, and *El mes colombino.* The cover from an issue of the first of these is reproduced in Ibid., p. 11.

14. For a photo of the infant Falla in the arms of his nursemaid, see Ibid., p. 9.

15. *Obra completa de Federico García Lorca*, 2nd ed. (Madrid: Aguilar, 1977), 1:1007.

16. Lorca used to relate with great enthusiasm how,
    one day, Falla did not permit his servant to bolt
    the doors against two escapees from a nearby
    prison. (Francisco García Lorca, *Federico y su
    mundo*, 2nd. ed. [Madrid: Alianza, 1981], p. 150.)
17. Raquel de Castro, who knew Falla during his seven
    years in Argentina, recalls how he refused to move
    into a house because it had a "bad angel" (*mal
    ángel*). (Related to the author in Madrid on 14
    November 1981.) Ferrer Moratel, his doctor in
    Argentina, called him "a perfect gypsy" because
    of the seriousness with which he regarded such
    signs. (See his interview by Enrique Bramanti
    Jauregui in *La razón* [Buenos Aires], 1 November
    1948.)
18. *Diario de Cádiz*, 19 November 1885.
19. *Vida íntima*, p. 90.
20. *Federico*, p. 150.
21. Based on Jaime Pahissa, *Vida y obra de Manuel de
    Falla*, rev. ed. (Buenos Aires: Ricordi, 1956),
    pp. 182-83.
22. Falla to Ángel Barrios, 4 August 1919, quoted in
    Federico Sopeña Ibáñez, *"Atlántida": introducción
    a Manuel de Falla* (Madrid: Taurus, 1962), p. 61.
23. The most thorough discussion of Beethoven's rela-
    tionship with his father is Maynard Solomon's
    Beethoven (New York: Schirmer, 1977).
24. Viniegra, *Vida íntima*, p. 36.
25. Falla took the first prize in both the Ortíz y
    Cusso (a piano dealer) competition (4 May 1905)
    and an opera contest sponsored by the Royal Academy
    of Fine Arts (13 November 1905), for which he com-
    posed *La vida breve*.
26. Falla's school records are reproduced in Orozco,
    Biografía, p. 16.
27. Viniegra, *Vida íntima*, p. 62.
28. See *El diario de Cádiz*, 28 March 1898, and concert
    posters dated 10 September 1899 and 16 September
    1900, reproduced in Orozco, *Biografía*, p. 18.
29. Cf. Manuel de Falla, *Obras desconocidas*, 3 vols.,
    ed. Enrique Franco (Madrid: Unión Musical Española,
    1980); and Manuel de Falla, *Inéditos de Manuel de
    Falla*, RCA SRL-2466.

30. "Felipe Pedrell," *La revue musicale* 4 (February 1923): 1-11.

31. For the complete conditions of the Royal Academy of Arts competition see Guillermo Fernández Shaw, *Larga historia de "La vida breve": años de lucha de Manuel de Falla* (Madrid: Sociedad General de Autores Españoles, 1964), pp. 22-24.

32. Ibid., pp. 27-30.

33. As we delve into Falla's experiences with the music merchants of Paris it will become increasingly clear that he made an unconscious connection between their occupation and that of his father (a businessman), to whom he did not want to be indebted.

34. Demarquez and Pahissa state that he arrived in the summer of 1907; Campoamor González specifies May, and Orozco July. (Suzanne Demarquez, *Manuel de Falla*, trans. and notes by Juan-Eduardo Cirlot [Barcelona: Editorial Labor, 1968], p. 44; Pahissa, *Vida y obra*, p. 47; Campoamor González, *Falla 1876-1946*, p. 51; Orozco, *Biografía*, pp. 39-40.)

35. Quoted in Mariano Pérez Gutiérrez, *Falla y Turina: a través de su epistolario* (Madrid: Editorial Alpuerto, 1982), p. 102.

36. Falla to his parents, quoted in Orozco, *Biografía*, pp. 42-44, and Falla to Carlos Fernández Shaw, quoted in Fernández Shaw, *Larga historia*, pp. 76-79.

37. *Falla 1876-1946*, p. 52.

38. *Manuel de Falla*, p. 45.

39. Falla to his parents, 16 August 1907, quoted in Orozco, *Biografía*, p. 43.

40. Falla to Fernández Shaw, 16 August 1907, quoted in Fernández Shaw, *Larga historia*, pp. 77-79.

41. *Vida y obra*, p. 49.

42. Falla to Fernández Shaw, 31 May 1910, quoted in Fernández Shaw, *Larga historia*, pp. 96-100. My translation is based on a version of this transcription, corrected by a comparison with the facsimile on p. 114. In the final paragraph on p. 97 (transcription), "Ya" should be deleted, "hora" should read "tuve," and "ser" should read "ver."

43. Falla to his family, 16 August 1907, quoted in Orozco, *Biografía*, p. 43.
44. Ibid.
45. Falla to Fernández Shaw, 5 February 1908, quoted in Fernández Shaw, *Larga historia*, pp. 79–80.
46. Falla to Fernández Shaw, 11 July 1908, quoted in ibid., pp. 85–87.
47. Falla to Fernández Shaw, 10 May 1910, quoted in ibid., pp. 94–96. Ronald Crichton (*Manuel de Falla: Descriptive Catalogue of his Works* [London: J. & W. Chester, Ltd., 1976], p. 20) mistakenly postulates "late in 1910" as the date of this work's premiere.
48. Falla to Fernández Shaw, 31 May 1910, quoted in Fernández Shaw, *Larga historia* pp. 97–100.
49. Milliet's role in the opera's publication is outlined by Falla in two letters to his librettist's widow, Cecilia de Yturralde, dated 12 October 1912 and 16 December 1912, quoted in ibid., pp. 117–20.
50. Pahissa, *Vida y obra*, p. 55.
51. Ibid., p. 43.
52. Pahissa, who could have easily submitted his proofs to Falla (whom he often visited) for correction, chose not to do so. Instead he held on to his manuscript, publishing it immediately after Falla's death: the Prologue to the First Edition is dated October 1946 (Falla died in November), but his death is lamented in the Epilogue.
53. See, for example, Demarquez, *Manuel de Falla*, p. 52, and two articles in *Ritmo*, no. 467 (December 1976): José Luis García del Busto, "Falla, perfil biográfico," p. 11, and Manuel Chapa Brunet, "El silencio," p. 68.
54. "¿Cómo son la nueva juventud española?" *La gaceta literaria* (Madrid), 1 February 1929, p. 1.
55. The most extreme in this regard is Adolfo F. Masciopinto, (*El nacionalismo musical en Manuel de Falla* [Santa Fe: Ministerio de Educación, 1952]).
56. "Los cármenes de Granada," *ABC* (Madrid), 2 January 1955.
57. "[Falla's] Psychoneurosis" in *Mi recuerdo humano de Manuel de Falla* (Granada: Universidad de Granada, 1980), pp. 34–46.

58. "Manuel's Family in Paris," in *Vida íntima*, pp. 87-96.
59. Falla to his family, 13 January 1909, quoted in Orozco, *Biografía*, pp. 49-50.
60. Obdulia Garzón to Joaquín Turina (her fiancé), 29 January 1908, quoted in Pérez Gutiérrez, *Falla y Turina*, p. 43.
61. Falla to Fernández Shaw, 14 November 1908, quoted in Fernández Shaw, *Larga historia*, pp. 89-90.
62. Attributed in Pérez Gutiérrez, *Falla y Turina*, p. 40; Ronald Crichton, *Catalogue*, p. 15, and *Falla*, BBC Music Guides (London: BBC, 1982), p. 17; and others. Falla originally lived in the Hôtel Kleber, but vacated it on 16 November 1907 because his piano playing bothered Turina, who also lived there (Turina to Obdulia Garzón, 15 November 1907, quoted in Pérez Gutiérrez, *Falla y Turina*, p. 39). He then lived at 20 rue Chalgrin, XVIe, until the summer of 1908, when he resided in Neuilly sur Seine (Falla to Fernández Shaw, 21 August 1908, quoted in Fernández Shaw, *Larga historia*, pp. 87-89).
63. Falla to Cecilia de Yturralde, 26 December 1911, quoted in Fernández Shaw, *Larga historia*, pp. 115-16. Falla had previously traveled to Brussels in the summer of 1908—from 12 to 15 or 16 July—possibly for the same reason. (See Falla to Fernández Shaw, 11 July 1908, quoted in ibid., pp. 85-87, and Falla to Turina, 12 July 1908, quoted in Pérez Gutiérrez, *Falla y Turina*, p. 129.)
64. The concert poster is reproduced in Pérez Gutiérrez, *Falla y Turina*, p. 47.
65. Mosco Carner, *Puccini: a Critical Biography*, 2nd ed. (London: Duckworth, 1974), p. 193.
66. Paul Milliet had assured Fernández Shaw that the French version of the opera would be performed during the 1910-11 season of the Opéra-Comique. See letter dated 26 May 1910, quoted in Fernández Shaw, *Larga historia*, p. 111.
67. A complete account of the opera's publication and early performance history is contained in Falla's letters to Cecilia de Yturralde, transcribed in ibid., pp. 115-58.

68. Falla to Cecilia de Yturralde, 31 July 1914, quoted in ibid., p. 151.

69. See Turina to Falla, 11 August 1914, quoted in Pérez Gutiérrez, *Falla y Turina*, p. 103, which refers to Falla's previous letter, now lost.

70. The most detailed account of Falla's *Wanderjahr* is contained in María Martínez Sierra, *Gregorio y yo: medio siglo de colaboración* (México, D.F.: Gandesa, 1953).

71. *El heraldo de Madrid*, 15 November 1914, quoted in Fernández Shaw, *Larga historia*, pp. 68-69.

72. Indeed an entire monograph has been devoted to his role in this process: Burnett James, *Manuel de Falla and the Spanish Musical Renaissance* (London: Gollancz, 1979).

73. "Nuestra música," *Música* (Madrid), 1 June 1917, quoted in Federico Sopeña Ibáñez, ed., *Escritos sobre música y músicos*, 3rd ed. (Madrid: Espasa-Calpe, 1972), p. 60.

74. December 1920, pp. 206-10.

75. "Notes sur Ravel," *La revue musicale* 20 (March 1939): 81-86.

76. Falla, "Felipe Pedrell," p. 5.

77. Martínez Sierra, *Gregorio y yo*, pp. 133-34.

78. Falla to Fernández Shaw, 31 May 1910, quoted above.

79. *Manuel de Falla*, p. 260 and *Catalogue*, p. 27.

80. See Falla to his family, 13 January 1909, quoted above, in which he asks his parents to send him the unfinished score of *Nights in the Gardens of Spain*.

81. The only extant autograph material for this body of works is a draft of *El corregidor y la molinera*, which we shall discuss below.

82. The most important sources for information about the production of these works are advertisements and reviews in contemporary Spanish newspapers. Cf. the list of Falla's works in Chapter II.

83. Cf. G.W. Hopkins, "Paul Dukas," *The New Grove Dictionary of Music*, ed. Stanley Sadie, 5:692.

84. Pahissa, *Vida y obra*, pp. 104-9, compares the contents of the two works, but it is quite unreliable because the author has to rely on his memory (or perhaps Falla's memory) of a performance of *El corregidor y la molinera* that he heard in 1907.

85. See Andrew Budwig, "The Evolution of Manuel de Falla's *The Three-Cornered Hat*, 1916-20," *Journal of Musicological Research* (Spring 1984): 191-212.
86. So popular was the Ballets Russes that accounts of each performance were featured on the front pages of Madrid's newspapers during its two seasons (June 1916 and 1917) there.
87. Falla to Floro M. Ugarte (Director of the Teatro Colón in Buenos Aires), 21 July 1941.
88. Contained on the verso of the 25-page musical draft for Part 1 (dated 8 August 1916) and the 43-page musical draft for Part 2 (dated 16 December 1916) of *El corregidor y la molinera*. Parts of this scenario are transcribed in Spanish and English in Budwig, "The Three-Cornered Hat."
89. *El sombrero de tres picos* of Pedro Antonio de Alarcón (1833-91).
90. *Vida y obra*, p. 108.
91. Leonide Massine, *My Life in Ballet*, ed. Phyllis Hartrell and Robert Rubens (London: Macmillan, 1968), p. 115.
92. The first and last pages of his contract with Diaghilev are reproduced in Pablo Picasso, *Designs for "The Three-Cornered Hat" (le Tricorne)*, ed. Parmenia Migel (New York: Dover, 1978), p. vi.
93. Massine, *My Life*, pp. 116-22.
94. See Picasso, *Designs*.
95. See Stravinsky to Ansermet, 30 May 1919, quoted in Robert Craft, ed., *Stravinsky: Selected Correspondence* I (New York: Alfred Knopf, 1982), pp. 136-37.
96. Falla to María Martínez Sierra, 4 and 19 June 1917.
97. Falla to Harry Kling (director of J. & W. Chester, Ltd.), 29 April 1922.
98. Diaghilev to Falla, 29 April 1923.
99. María del Carmen de Falla's account in Viniegra, *Vida íntima*, p. 102.
100. Falla to Zuloaga, 17 April 1919, quoted in Federico Sopeña Ibáñez, ed., *Correspondencia entre Falla y Zuloaga, 1915-1942* (Granada: Ayuntamiento de Granada, 1982), unpaged.

101. See Falla to Zuloaga, undated and 16 June 1919, quoted in ibid.

102. Dedicated to Juan Gisbert Padró, December 1923, reproduced in Demarquez, *Falla*, p. 91.

103. Martínez Sierra, *Gregorio y yo*, p. 135. Falla himself must have felt torn between the love of two such women at some point in his life. The two women to whom he was closest in infancy were his mother, a paradigm of sensitive spirituality, and his nursemaid, a simple gypsy who satisfied his physical needs. As a shy and pious young man, Manuel sublimated any physical interests he might have had ... until he met his cousin María Ledesma, the daughter of his mother's sister Emilia. Falla fell in love with María while he was living with her family in Madrid (1897–98). According to Viniegra (*Vida íntima*, pp. 184–86), her refusal of his marriage offer was the cause of his life-long celibacy. This testimony was corroborated by a more reliable source, Ms. Isabel Luzuriaga, María's daughter (in a conversation with Andrew Budwig in Madrid on Christmas Day, 1981). According to Ms. Luzuriaga, her mother was indeed the only woman that Falla ever considered marrying, and when the Fallas and the Luzuriagas met by chance years later in Argentina (1939), Manuel and María (whom he called Maruca) became close friends. Many excerpts from the Falla–Luzuriaga correspondence are transcribed in Andrew Budwig, *Manuel de Falla's "Atlántida": an Historical and Analytical Study* (Ph.D. Dissertation, University of Chicago, 1984).

104. Excerpts from the Falla–Landowska correspondence are transcribed in ibid. An account of Falla's search for harpsichords on which to perform his works is contained in his letters to Segismundo Romero, transcribed in Falla, *Cartas a Segismundo Romero*, Pascual Recuero, ed. (Granada: Ayuntamiento de Granada, 1976).

105. After *The Three-Cornered Hat*, he never worked with a collaborator. Granted the painter José María Sert was going to design the costumes and sets for Falla's cantata *Atlántida*, but there is no evidence that Sert ever actively contributed to the work.

106. Falla's biographers have disregarded the devastating effect of Spain's political and civil strife on his work. Although poor health did indeed hinder his progress (several authors, especially Jiménez, dwell on this point), Falla's ailments were in turn exacerbated by any small disagreement that he might have had with a student, a friend, or with government policy. The following survey of Spanish history is based primarily on Richard Carr, *Modern Spain, 1875-1980* (Oxford: Oxford University Press, 1980).

107. E.g., in Paris in March 1926, May 1927, and March 1928.

108. See Juan Gisbert Padró, "Origens de *Atlántida*," *ABC* (Madrid) 29 December 1960.

109. For a thorough treatment of this subject see Budwig, *Manuel de Falla's "Atlántida."*

110. The first of his letters in which he mentions this problem are those to his student Ernesto Halffter, dated 31 May and 28 June 1928.

111. Falla first mentions these more serious maladies in a letter to Adolfo Salazar dated 31 January 1930.

112. Falla to John B. Trend, 4 May 1931, quoted in Sopeña Ibáñez, *Atlántida*, pp. 76-77.

113. Quoted in English in Carr, *Spain*, p. 117.

114. Falla to John B. Trend, 20 May 1931, quoted in Sopeña Ibáñez, *Atlántida*, pp. 77-78.

115. Falla to Ríos, 13 August 1932.

116. *La unión*, 8 June 1932.

117. Falla to José Pemán, 18 September 1936.

118. Falla to Sert, 10 November 1928, transcribed in Demarquez, *Manuel de Falla*, pp. 246-250.

119. The earliest version of the "Salve" in the *Atlántida* autographs is found on folio C39v and dated 27 February 1932. The first version of Falla's will is dated February 1932.

120. See Falla to Gaspar Pintado, 4 December 1929, quoted in Budwig, *Manuel de Falla's "Atlántida."*

121. María del Carmen Falla to Padre Thomas, 18 January 1933, quoted in Juan María Thomas, *Manuel de Falla en la isla* (Palma: Capella Clàssica, 1948), pp. 43-44.

122. Although Falla composed and adapted several short works for choir and composed a brass fanfare during these two years, it is evident that he did not make any progress on his *Atlántida* (See Budwig, *Manuel de Falla's Atlántida*).
123. Falla to Zuloaga, 10 November 1934, quoted in Sopeña Ibáñez, *Correspondencia*.
124. Two passages from that number contained on folio A78 of the autographs are dated 13 February and 23 April 1935. Falla also mentions the "Salve" in letters to Leopoldo Matos (his attorney and friend), 17 May 1935, and Sert, 2 August 1935.
125. Falla to Padre Thomas, 11 February 1935, quoted in Thomas, *Isla*, pp. 305-6.
126. Transcribed in Campoamor González, *Falla 1876-1946*, pp. 217ff.
127. E.g., "Soneto a Córdoba" (1927) after Góngora, "Balada de Mallorca" (1933)--an adaptation of a Chopin ballad with text by Jacinto Verdaguer, etc.
128. Falla to María Luzuriaga, 25 January 1946.

CHAPTER II

CHRONOLOGICAL LIST OF FALLA'S COMPOSITIONS

Until now the most detailed catalogue of Falla's
music, and of transcriptions and arrangements of his
works by other composers, has been Ronald Crichton's
Manuel de Falla: Descriptive Catalogue of his Work (see
item 383). The work list in Enrique Franco's Falla
article in *The New Grove Dictionary of Music and Musicians* (see item 152) is also useful in spite of its
inaccuracies. The other secondary sources consulted
for information on unpublished works are cited by item
and page number in parentheses at the end of each entry.
These sources include facsimiles of scores and early
concert programs as well as correspondence or personal
accounts concerning dates of composition, publication,
and performance.
This catalogue differs from others in that it is
both complete and chronological and, wherever possible,
is based on primary sources: the correspondence and
autograph score housed in the Falla family archives.
Each entry includes: date of composition, description
of work, place and date of premiere, place and date of
publication, and location of the autograph score. The
designation "MS" indicates that the original manuscript
copy of the score is in the archives of the Falla family; otherwise, if it is extant, the autograph is owned
by the publisher or by a third party, as indicated.

1. *El Conde de Villamediana.* c. 1885–87. A youthful
    attempt at opera seria, based on poems by the Duque
    de Rivas (1791–1865). Lost. (66:15, 77:24, 271:
    297)

2. *Gavotte et Musette.* c. 1885–87. Two pieces for
    piano solo in the style of Bach. Lost. (66:15,
    271:297)

3. *Melodia.* 19 June 1897. For violoncello and piano,
    ternary song form in the style of Brahms. Cadiz:
    salon of Manuel Quirell, 18 August 1899. Madrid:
    Unión Musical Española, 1980 (see item 375). MS.

4. *Romanza.* 1897. For violoncello and piano, in a
    late-Romantic style. Cadiz: salon of Salvador
    Viniegra, 14 July 1899. Madrid: Unión Musical
    Española, 1980 (see item 375). MS.

5. *Cuarteto.* c. 1898–99. Two movements for piano,
    violin, viola, and violoncello entitled: "Andante
    tranquilo" and "Bailable." Cadiz: Teatro Cómico,
    10 September 1899. MS. (60:30, 66:16, 271:297)

6. *Mireya.* c. 1898–99. Two movements for flute,
    piano, violin, viola, and violoncello, after the
    fifth poem, "Canto a Ródano," from the *Mireya* of
    F. Mistral (1830–1914). MS. (60:30, 66:16, 271:
    298–99)

7. *Nocturno.* c. 1898–99. For piano solo. Cadiz:
    Teatro Cómico, 10 September 1899. Madrid: Unión
    Musical Española, 1940, 1980 (see item 375). MS.

8. *Serenata Andaluza.* c. 1898–99. For violin and
    piano. Cadiz: Teatro Cómico, 10 September 1899.
    MS. (60:30, 77:18, 271:299)

9. *Canción.* 2 April 1900. For piano solo, in a
    surprisingly cosmopolitan style somewhere between
    that of Chopin and Satie. Madrid: Unión Musical
    Española, 1980 (see item 375). MS.

10. *Dos rimas*. 1900. Two songs for mezzo-soprano
     and piano after the poems, "Olas gigantes" and
     "Dios mío, que solo se quedan los muertos" by
     Gustavo Becquer (1836-70). Operatic, but with a
     few Spanish arabesques and open fifths. Madrid:
     Unión Musical Española, 1980 (see item 375). MS.

11. *La casa de tócame Roque*. 1900. *Zarzuela* in one
     act, libretto in MS. (291:297-98)

12. *Preludios*. 1900. A bel canto setting of verses
     by the popular Basque poet Antonio de Trueba (1819-
     99), for mezzo-soprano and piano. Madrid: Unión
     Musical Española, 1980 (see item 375.) MS.

13. *Serenata andaluza*. 1900. For piano solo, unre-
     lated to the work by the same name for violin and
     piano. Cadiz: Real Academia de Santa Cecilia, 16
     September 1900. Madrid: Faustino Fuentes, [1901];
     Madrid: A. Fassio, [1935]; New York: G. Schirmer,
     [1940]. MS.

14. *Tus ojillos negros*. 1900. For mezzo-soprano and
     piano, on a sentimental text by Cristóbal Castro.
     Achieved great acclaim in America during World
     War II. Madrid: Faustino Fuentes, [1901]; New
     York: Edward B. Marks Music Corp., [1943]; Madrid:
     Unión Musical Española, 1940; 1980 (see item 375).
     MS.

15. *Vals Capricho*. 1900. For piano solo. Madrid:
     Faustino Fuentes, [1901]; Madrid: Unión Musical
     Española, 1940. MS lost.

16. *Cortejo de gnomos*. 4 March 1901. A character
     piece for piano solo, in the style of Grieg. Ma-
     drid: Unión Musical Española, 1980 (see item 375).
     MS.

17. *Limosna de amor*. 1901. *Zarzuela* in one act, li-
     bretto by Jackson Veyan. Lost. (271:297-98)

18. *Serenata.* 2 April 1901. For piano solo. MS. (271:61-66)

19. *Los amores de Inés.* 1902. *Zarzuela* in one act, libretto by Emilio Dugi: Inés is plagued by a variety of suitors until her true love Juan is released from jail. Madrid: Teatro Cómico, 12 April 1902. Madrid: Unión Musical Española, 1965.

20. *Allegro de concierto.* c. 1902-3. For piano solo, submitted to a jury of the National Conservatory in Madrid under the countersign "X" as the final for the composition course there. Madrid: Ateneo de Madrid, 15 May 1905. MS. (77:16, 271:71-80)

21. *El corneta de órdenes.* c. 1902-3. *Zarzuela* in 3 acts, written in collaboration with the then established composer Amadeo Vives (1871-1932). Lost. (271:297-98)

22. *La cruz de Malta.* c. 1902-3. *Zarzuela* in one act, written in collaboration with Amadeo Vives. Lost. (271: 297-98)

23. *La vida breve.* 1904-5. Opera in 2 acts, libretto by Carlos Fernández Shaw. The setting is the gypsy quarter of Granada. Salud is seduced by Paco, who is already engaged to marry a wealthy girl of his own class, Carmela. Paco's deceit is avenged by Salud herself, who exposes their affair at his wedding party and then falls dead at his feet. Submitted on 31 March 1905 under the countersign "San Fernando" to the Royal Academy of Fine Arts who was sponsoring an opera competition. Although it won first prize, *La vida breve* was not performed, as had been promised, and thus Falla took it to Paris in 1907 where he eventually made his name with it. Nice: Casino Municipal, 1 April 1913; Paris: Opéra-Comique, 7 January 1914. Paris: Max Eschig, 1913 (piano-vocal score with French translation by Paul Milliet); 1925 (libretto with English version by Frederick H. Martens); 1982 (full study score). MS owned by the City of Granada.

24. *Pièces espagnoles.* 1902-8. Four pieces for piano
     solo: "Aragonesa," "Cubana," "Montanesa," and
     "Andaluza." Paris: Salle Érard, 23 March 1909.
     Paris: Durand et Cie., 1909; Madrid: Unión Musical
     Española, 1952; Philadelphia: Elkan-Vogel, 1962.

25. *Trois mélodies.* 1909. For mezzo-soprano and pi-
     ano, on poems by Théophile Gautier (1811-72):
     "Les colombes," "Chinoiserie," "Séguidille."
     Paris: Société Independent Musical, 4 May 1910.
     Paris: Rouart, Lerolle et Cie., 1910. New York:
     International Music Corporation, 1954 (with English
     trans. by Edith Brain).

26. *Amanecer.* 1914. Incidental music for this play
     by Gregorio Martínez Sierra (1881-1947). Lost.
     (64:49)

27. *Oración de las madres que tienen a sus hijos en
     brazos.* December 1914. For mezzo-soprano and
     piano. The text by G. Martínez Sierra is a prayer
     for mothers who do not want their sons to become
     soldiers. Madrid: Sociedad Nacional de Música,
     8 February 1915. Madrid: Unión Musical Española,
     1980 (see item 375). MS.

28. *El amor brujo.* 1914-15. Ballet in one act, sce-
     nario by G. Martínez Sierra: Candelas, a gypsy
     girl, is haunted by the ghost of her former lover.
     Her friend Lucía uses her charms to divert the
     spirit, thereby permitting Carmelo to win over
     Candelas. Madrid: Teatro Lara, 2 April 1915 (orig-
     inal version). MS lost, unique copy of the origi-
     nal version housed in the Library of Congress.
     Madrid: Sociedad Nacional de Música, 28 March,
     1916 (revised version). London: J. & W. Chester,
     1921, 1949 (piano-vocal score with complete sce-
     nario); 1924 (full study score).

29. *Siete canciones populares españoles.* 1914-15.
     Settings of traditional songs, for mezzo-soprano
     and piano: "El paño moruno," "Seguidilla murciana,"
     "Asturiana," "Jota," "Nana," "Canción," and "Polo."

Madrid: Ateneo de Madrid, 14 January 1915. Paris:
Max Eschig, 1922 (with French trans. by Paul
Milliet); New York: Associated Music Publishers,
1943 (with English translation by Elaine de
Sinçay).

30. *Othello*. June 1915. Incidental music for G.
Martínez Sierra's production of Shakespeare's trag-
edy in translation. Barcelona: Teatro de Nove-
dades, 1915. Lost. (64:49)

31. *Canción andaluza: El pan de Ronda*. 18 December
1915. For mezzo-soprano and piano, with text by
G. Martínez Sierra. A tribute to the integrity
of the Andalusians--and their bread. Madrid: Unión
Musical Española, 1980 (see item 375). MS.

32. *Noches en los jardines de España*. 1907-16. For
piano and orchestra in 3 movements: "En el
Generalife," "Danza lejana," and "En los jardines
de la Sierra de Córdoba." The piano is used solo-
istically in much the same way that Stravinsky
used it in *Petrushka* (1911). Madrid: Teatro Real,
9 April 1916. Paris: Max Eschig, 1922.

33. *Soleá*. 1916. For voice and guitar. Incidental
music for a play by G. Martínez Sierra entitled
La pasión. MS. (64:49)

34. *El corregidor y la molinera*. 1916-17. Pantomime
in two tableaux, scenario by G. Martínez Sierra
after novel by Pedro Antonio de Alarcón (1833-91).
The instrumental ensemble for this precursor of
The Three-Cornered Hat is the same as that of the
original version of *El amor brujo*: flute, oboe,
clarinet, bassoon, 2 horns, trumpet, and strings.
Madrid: Teatro Eslava, 7 April 1917. London:
J. & W. Chester, 1982. MS.

35. *The Three-Cornered Hat*. 1917-19. Ballet in 2
parts, adapted for Diaghilev's Ballets Russes from
the more melodramatic and provincial *El corregidor
y la molinera*. The story is same as that of Hugo

Wolf's *Der Corregidor*: The *corregidor* (civil governor) becomes enamored of the miller's wife and arrests her husband on trumped-up charges in order to have her to himself. However, because he is a doddering old fool, everything goes wrong and his beloved ends up chastising him while her husband succeeds in seducing the wife of the *corregidor*. Original production choreographed by Massine, with costumes and set by Picasso. London: Alhambra Theatre, 22 July 1919. London: J. & W. Chester, 1921 (piano-vocal score with complete scenario); 1925, 1949 (full study score).

36. *Fuego fatuo*. May–September 1918. Unfinished comic opera in 3 acts, libretto by G. Martínez Sierra. Based on melodies from 21 works of Chopin (listed in item 383). Suite adapted from Acts 1 and 3 by Antonio Ros Marbá, performed in Granada: Festival de Granada, 1 July 1976. MS. (77:41)

37. *Fantasía Bética*. January–May 1919. For piano solo, commissioned by Artur Rubinstein (as was the contemporary *Piano-Rag-Music* of Stravinsky). New York: [?], 20 January 1920. London, J. & W. Chester, 1922; 1950. MS in the British Library.

38. *Hommage "Le tombeau de Claude Debussy."* 1920. For guitar solo, quotes from Debussy's "Soirée dans Grenade." Paris: Société Independent de Musique, 24 January 1921. *La revue musicale*, December 1920 (see item 317); London: J. & W. Chester, 1921.

39. *Fanfare pour une fête*. 1921. For two trumpets, timpani, and snare drum. London: Eugene Goosens, 22 October 1921. *Fanfare* 1, August 1921 (see item 290). MS owned by Ernesto Halffter.

40. *Orchestral Suites from "The Three-Cornered Hat."* 1919–21. "Scenes and Dances" from Part 1 and "Three Dances" from Part 2. The vocal solos contained in the original ballet are elided, as is the introductory hand-clapping. London: J. & W. Chester, 1925, 1942, 1962.

41. *Cante a los romeros de Volga*. March 1922. For
    piano solo. This haunting arrangement anticipates
    the dense chordal style of *Pour le tombeau de Paul
    Dukas*. Madrid: Unión Musical Española, 1980 (see
    item 375). MS.

42. *Auto de los Reyes Magos*. 1922. Setting of medie-
    val melodies from Pedrell's *Cancionero* (see item
    114) for clarinet, violin, and piano. Performed
    with Stravinsky's arrangement, for the same en-
    semble, of *L'histoire du soldat* to accompany puppet
    plays of Lorca. Granada: Lorca's home, 6 January
    1923. Lost. (items 103, 184, 190, 195)

43. *El retablo de Maese Pedro*. 1919-22. Puppet play
    adapted from Cervantes' *Quijote*, Book 2, chapters
    25-26, by Falla. Don Quijote and Sancho (repre-
    sented by actors or large marionettes) watch Maese
    Pedro re-enact the ancient story of Melisenda's
    rescue from the Moors by Don Gayferos, a knight
    in Charlemagne's court. The hand-puppet play on
    stage is narrated by a *trujamán* (boy soprano) who
    is so successful at bringing his characters to
    life that Don Quijote forgets himself and joins
    in the battle between Christian and Moorish pup-
    pets. Seville: Teatro San Fernando, 23 March 1923
    (concert); Paris: theater of the Princess de
    Polignac, 25 June 1923 (staged). London: J. & W.
    Chester, 1924 (piano-vocal score with detailed
    stage directions--English trans. John B. Trend
    and French trans. Jean Aubry); 1924 (full study
    score).

44. *Psyché*. 1924. For mezzo-soprano, flute, harp,
    violin, viola, and violoncello, on a poem by Jean
    Aubry (1882-1949). Falla describes an imaginary
    setting in the preface: a court concert in the
    Tocador de la Reina of the Alhambra Palace during
    the visit of Philip V and his queen, Elisabeth
    Farnese, in 1730. Barcelona: [?], December 1924.
    London: J. & W. Chester, 1927.

45. *Concerto.* 1923-26. For harpsichord or piano, flute, oboe, clarinet, violin, and violoncello in three movements: Allegro, Lento, Vivace. Barcelona: Asociación de Música de Cámera, 5 November 1926. Paris: Max Eschig, 1928.

46. *Soneto a Córdoba.* 1927. For soprano and harp or piano, on a poem by Luis de Góngora (1561-1627). Paris: Salle Pleyel, 14 May 1927. First appeared with a poem by Lorca, a drawing by Picasso, etc., in an issue of *Litoral* (see item 325) honoring the tricentenary of Góngora's death. London: Oxford University Press, 1932; J. & W. Chester, 1956.

47. *Overture to "Il barbiere de Siviglia"* (Rossini). 1927. Re-orchestration with the trombone parts suppressed. Paris: Theatre des Champs-Élysées, 17 June 1927. Lost. (271:254)

48. *El gran teatro del mundo.* May 1927. Incidental music for this *auto sacramental* of Lope de Vega (1562-1635). Employs melodies from Pedrell's *Cancionero* (see item 117). Granada: University of Granada, 1928. MS owned by Ernesto Halffter. (184)

49. *Invocatio ad Individuam Trinitatem.* 1928. For unaccompanied 4-part choir, in the style of Tomás Luis Victoria (1540-1613). San Sebastian: Orfeón Donostiarra, 4 September 1932. MS.

50. *L'amfiparnasso.* 1932. Arrangement for four-part unaccompanied choir of the first madrigal in this set by Orazio Vecchi (1550-1604). Palma de Mallorca: Capella Real de la Almudaina, 12 June 1934. MS.

51. *Balada de Mallorca.* 1933. For unaccompanied 4-part choir. Adaptation of the Andantino sections of Chopin's Ballade in F, Op. 38. Text from the epic, *L'Atlàntida* of Jacint Verdaguer (1845-1902). Mallorca: Monasterio de Valldemosa, 21 May 1933. Milan: G. Ricordi & C., 1975.

52. *Fanfare sobre el nombre de E. F. Arbós.* 1933-34.
     For horns, trumpets, and percussion. Based on
     the *soggetto cavato* E-F-A-Re(D)-B-Do(C)-Sol(G) in
     honor of Arbós on his seventieth birthday. Madrid:
     Teatro Calderón, 20 March 1934. MS.

53. *Pour le tombeau de Paul Dukas.* December 1935.
     For piano solo. First appeared in *La revue musi-
     cale*, May-June 1936 (see item 321). Milan: G.
     Ricordi & C., 1974.

54. *Canto de marcha para los soldados españoles.* 1937.
     For unison male voices, poem by José María Pemán
     (see item 273). This melody is an adaptation of
     the "Canto de los almogávares" from Pedrell's op-
     era *Los Pirineos*. Lost. (items 145-47)

55. *Homenajes.* 1935-39. For orchestra, in 4 move-
     ments: Fanfare sobre el nombre de E.F. Arbós, à
     Claude Debussy, à Paul Dukas, Pedrelliana. The
     first three, composed between 1920 and 1935, were
     orchestrated by Falla during the Civil War. The
     final movement, based on passages from Pedrell's
     opera *La Celestina*, was originally written for
     the Barcelona International Exposition (1936) but
     was not completed in time for a performance there.
     Buenos Aires: Teatro Colón, 18 November 1939.
     London: J. & W. Chester and Milan: G. Ricordi &
     C., 1953.

56. *Fifteenth and Sixteenth Century Villancicos.* 1941-
     44. Adapted for accompanied 4-part choir with
     instrumental interludes: "Que es de ti desconso-
     lada" and "Tan buen ganadico" of Juan del Encina
     (1446-1534), "Ora sus" of Juan Escobar (1465-1535),
     "Prado verde y florida" of Francisco Guerrero
     (1528-99), "Emendemus melius" of Cristóbal Morales
     (1512-53), "O magnum mysterium," "Tenebrae factae
     sunt," "Miserere mei," "Vexilla regis," "In festo
     Sancti Jacobi," and "Vidi speciosam" of Victoria.
     Most of these works are transcribed in Pedrell's
     Cancionero (see item 117). Buenos Aires: Teatro
     Colón, 21 May 1945. MS.

57. *Atlántida*. 1927-1946. Unfinished scenic cantata
     in 3 parts with a prologue, libretto by Falla based
     on *L'Atlàntida* of Jacint Vedaguer (1845-1902):
     Out of the destruction of decadent Atlantis Spain
     is born. Just as Hercules (in this account) is
     the hero responsible for this miracle, Columbus,
     guided by the Divine Will, founds a New Atlantis.
     Barcelona: Teatro del Liceo, 24 November 1961
     (suite); Milan: Teatro alla Scala, 1962 (complete).
     Milan: G. Ricordi & C., 1958 (libretto); 1961
     (suite); 1962 (full and piano-vocal scores). A
     "definitive" version was performed at the Lucerne
     Festival on 9 September 1976, and yet another var-
     iant has been recorded (see item 372).

CHAPTER III

GENERAL STUDIES ON FALLA AND HIS PERIOD

1. *Biographies and Comprehensive Studies*

58. Arizaga, Rodolfo. *Manuel de Falla*. Buenos Aires: Goyanarte, 1961. 166 pp.

      A biographical study but with an emphasis on the description of individual works as isolated entities. Provides extensive information regarding important performances, critical reception, etc., for every composition.

59. Budwig, Andrew. "Manuel de Falla's *Atlántida*: an Historical and Analytical Study." Ph.D. Dissertation, University of Chicago, 1984. 474 pp.

      Answers the long-asked question--how much of *Atlántida* was completed by Falla?--by analyzing the autograph score of this posthumous cantata. A thorough biographical study of the composer's years of maturity (1926-46). Quotes extensively from unpublished correspondence housed in the private archives of the Falla family.

60. Campoamor González, Antonio. *Manuel de Falla, 1876-1946*. Madrid: Sedmay Ediciones, 1976. 216 pp.

      Synthesizes the material in Demarquez,

Orozco, Pahissa, and Viniegra (items 66, 77, 81, and 92) in a primarily chronological biography for the non-musician. Contains the text of Falla's will and several black-and-white photographs.

61. Campodónico, Luis. *Falla.* Translated by Françoise Avila. Collections microcosme, solfèges, no. 13. Paris: Editions du Seuil, 1959. 190 pp.

A basic biography with a particularly detailed account of Falla's Paris years (1907-14). Illustrated with an unusual assortment of photographs, dance-hall posters, and facsimilies of letters and musical scores. Contains a chronological table of events, a discography, and a work list.

62. Casanovas, José. *Manuel de Falla, cien años.* Barcelona: Ediciones de Nuevo Arte Thor, 1976. 94 pp.

Yet another derivative biography written in celebration of the centenary of Falla's birth. Includes a bibliography, work list, and chronological table of events.

63. Costas, Carlos José. *Falla: cincuenta años después del "Retablo."* Cadiz: Ediciones de la Caja de Ahorros de Cádiz, 1973. 48 pp.

Argues that Falla has been misrepresented, especially in the United States, as a result of his early works being performed with greater frequency than his later works.

64. Crichton, Ronald. *Falla.* BBC Music Guides. London: British Broadcasting Corporation, 1982. 104 pp.

A clear and concise chronological survey of Falla's life and works. Addresses several issues that are often avoided: for example, the matter of the will as an expression of the composer's dissatisfaction. Includes a generous number of musical examples.

65. Cúllar, José María de. *Falla: otro español universal.* Madrid: Ediciones PPC, 1968. 48 pp.

A brief, popular biography.

66. Demarquez, Suzanne. *Manuel de Falla.* Preface by Bernard Gavoty. Paris: Flammarion, 1963. 252 pp.

Combines music analyses of the major works with biographical material in a convincing manner. The music is explained in terms of possible folk influence rather than in absolute harmonic, rhythmic, or melodic terms. Reproduces letter to the painter, José María Sert (10 November 1928), in which Falla describes his initial conception of *Atlántida.* Fully documented, with bibliography and work list.

67. ————. *Manuel de Falla.* Translated and with an epilogue by Juan-Eduardo Cirlot. Nueva colección Labor, no. 83. Barcelona: Editorial Labor, 1968. 271 pp.

68. ————. *Manuel de Falla.* Translated by Salvator Attanasio. Philadelphia: Chilton Book Co., 1968. 253 pp.

The most comprehensive biography in English to date.

69. Franco, Enrique. *Manuel de Falla y su obra.* Madrid: Publicaciones Españolas, 1976. 63 pp.

Addresses in a summary manner Falla's esthetic and ethical views. Provides a selection of excerpts from his writings which are of interest in spite of the total lack of documentation.

70. Gauthier, André. *Manuel de Falla, l'homme et son
     oeuvre*. Paris: Seghers, 1966. 191 pp.

         Largely derivative, intended for the general
     reader. Divided into two parts describing the
     man and his music, respectively. Includes an
     extensive discography.

71. Jaenisch, Julio. *Manuel de Falla und die spanische
     Musik*. Zurich: Atlantis Verlag, 1952. 103 pp.

         A concise, general biography. Contains a
     translation of the "Soneto a Córdoba."

72. James, Burnett. *Manuel de Falla and the Spanish
     Musical Renaissance*. London: Victor Gollancz,
     Ltd., 1979. 172 pp.

         Attempts to define Falla's position as a
     national and international composer. Biographi-
     cal material follows a general introduction to
     Spanish music.

73. Jiménez, Luis. *Mi recuerdo humano de Manuel de
     Falla*. Presented at a conference of the Comisión
     Pro-Centenario de la Muerte de Manuel de Falla,
     28 April 1976. Granada: University of Granada,
     1980. 79 pp.

         An account of Falla's habits and beliefs
     by a contemporary. Kantian speculation inter-
     spersed with interesting facts about the com-
     poser's years in Granada.

74. Masciopinto, F. Adolfo. *El nacionalismo musical
     en Manuel de Falla*. Publicación de Extensión
     Universitaria, no. 75. Santa Fe: Ministerio de
     Educación de la Nación, Universidad Nacional
     del Litoral, 1952. 38 pp.

         A biography based on those of Pahissa,
     Roland Manuel, and Sagardia (see items 80, 84,
     and 87). Propagates the narrow official view

of Falla as a fervant Catholic and a patriotic
Spaniard, ignoring his liberal sentiments regarding the poor and the working class.

75. Molina Fajardo, Eduardo. *Manuel de Falla y el
    "cante jondo."* Granada: Universidad de Granada,
    1962. 250 pp.

    An important source for imformation about
    Falla's early years in Granada (1920-25), and
    especially with respect to the interest that he
    and his fellow artists took in the preservation
    of the ancient *cante jondo.* The bibliography
    cites a number of articles which refer specifi-
    cally to the "Concurso de Cante Jondo" that
    Falla, Lorca, and others organized. The edition
    reprinted for the centenary of the composer's
    birth (1976) contains authentic, full-color
    copies of the official poster and ticket for
    this competition held in Granada in 1922.

76. Orozco, Manuel. *Biografía completa de Manuel de
    Falla.* Colección las protagonistas de la his-
    toria, no. 21. Madrid: Ibérico Europea de Edi-
    ciones, 1970. 32 pp.

    Extracted from item 77, but with the addi-
    tion of several large color photographs of
    Falla's home in Granada, and with a chronological
    chart of important events.

77. ————. *Falla: biografía illustrada.* Barcelona:
    Ediciones Destino, 1968. 212 pp.

    A comprehensive biography, magnificently
    illustrated with photographs and facsimiles of
    posters, letters, and autograph scores. The
    author, who knew Falla personally, describes
    for the first time the debilitating effects of
    his tuberculosis. As in many other studies by
    Spanish writers, passing references are made to
    obscure personages; nevertheless, this is an
    invaluable source for the reader who is somewhat
    acquainted with the subject.

78. ————. *Falla y Granada*. Temas de nuestra Anda-
     lucía, no. 42. Granada: Caja de Ahorros de Gra-
     nada, 1976. 16 pp.

     A further condensed version of item 77,
     intended for the general reader.

79. Pahissa, Jaime. *Manuel de Falla, His Life and
     Works*. Translated by Jean Wagstaff. London:
     Museum Press, 1954. 190 pp.

     Includes a preface by Salvador de Madariaga
     lacking in the other editions (items 80 and 81)
     in which the childlike aspects of Falla's per-
     sonality are described.

80. ————. *Vida y obra de Manuel de Falla*. Buenos
     Aires: G. Ricordi & Co., 1947. 207 pp.

     Claims to be the only biography authorized
     by Falla. A loosely structured study of the
     man and his music (with abundant examples), un-
     documented and replete with anecdotal dialogues,
     some of which appear to be apocryphal. Contains
     errata attributed to Falla (for the pocket score
     of the *Harpsichord Concerto*) as well as a fac-
     simile of one letter and transcriptions of two
     others.

81. ————. *Vida y obra de Manuel de Falla*, rev. ed.
     Buenos Aires: G. Ricordi & Co., 1956. 223 pp.

     Same as item 80, but with an appendix con-
     taining transcriptions of the marginal notes
     that Falla made on the early drafts of this
     study.

82. Pahlen, Kurt. *Manuel de Falla und die Music in
     Spanien*. Berlin: O. Walter Olten, 1953. 264 p.

     The most complete biography in German. The
     author met Falla in 1943, maintaining an active
     correspondence with him during his last three

years. The opening chapters are an historical
survey of Spanish music.

83. ————. *Manuel de Falla y la música de España.*
Translated by Cristóbal Halffter. Madrid: Editor Nacional, 1960. 280 pp.

84. Roland-Manuel, Alexis. *Manuel de Falla.* Paris:
Éditions Cahiers d'Art, 1930. 64 pp.

The first biography of Falla, it has yet
to be eclipsed. The author, a musician-priest
who befriended him in Paris, offers insights into
his deeply religious personality. The original
edition, limited to a thousand copies, was reprinted in a limited edition of four hundred
copies by Editions d'Aujourd'hui, 1977.

85. ————. *Manuel de Falla.* Translated and with an
essay by Vicente Salas Viu. Buenos Aires: Editorial Losada, 1945. 146 pp.

The translator adds four pages to the original (item 82) to bring it up to date. In the
essay that follows, "Falla y el futuro de la
música española," it is posited that Falla was
a more "Spanish" composer than Esplá, Turina,
or Conrado del Campo.

86. Ruiz Tarrazona, Andrés. *Manuel de Falla: un camino
de ascesis.* Madrid: Real Musical, 1975. 88 pp.

A concise, readable biography with a work
list and chronological table of events.

87. Sagardia, Angel. *Manuel de Falla.* Madrid: Unión
Musical Española, 1946. 76 pp.

Apart from the much earlier work of Roland
Manuel (item 81), the only comprehensive study
of Falla completed before his death. Analyzes
several early works with an entire chapter devoted to the hitherto unknown *Los amores de*

Inés. Quotes extensively from contemporary journalistic criticism.

88. ————. *Vida y obra de Manuel de Falla*. Madrid: Escelicer, 1967. 190 pp.

An expanded version of item 87 with chapters dedicated to *Atlántida* and to Falla's death and burial in Cadiz. A work list, discography, and bibliography have also been added.

89. Sopeña Ibáñez, Federico. *Manuel de Falla y el mundo de la cultura española*. Madrid: Instituto de España, 1976. 82 pp.

An apology for the dictatorships of Primo de Rivera (1923–29) and Franco (1939–76). Falla's religiosity is presented as "proof" of his satisfaction with the policies of these regimes.

90. Thomas, Juan María. *Manuel de Falla en la isla*. Palma de Mallorca: Ediciones Capella Clàssica, 1947. 341 pp.

Recounts the two extended visits that Falla paid the author in Mallorca (1933–34). Its novelesque style alludes to the *Quijote*, with each chapter prefaced by a summary of its content, and likewise depicts the composer as a peculiar sort of knight errant. An important source, however, replete with factual information about specific performances and excerpts from Falla's letters to the author.

91. Trend, John Brand. *Manuel de Falla and Spanish Music*. New York: Knopf, 1934; reprint ed. St. Clair Shores, Mich.: Scholarly Press, 1977. 184 pp.

An intimate history by a friend of Falla. Introduced with a substantial explanation of Spanish folk music. The appendix contains a translation of the *Seven Popular Songs*.

92. Viniegra y Lasso, Juan J., with Martel Viniegra,
     Carmen and Carlos. *Vida íntima de Manuel de
     Falla*. Cadiz: Excma. Diputación Provincial y
     Ayuntamiento, Caja de Ahorros, Cámara Oficical
     de Comercio, Industria y Navigación, 1966.
     273 pp.

         As the title suggests, an intimate account
     of Falla's personal life. A childhood friend
     of the composer, the author is able to provide
     a myriad of details about Falla's love life (a
     subject rarely broached), family, and education.
     As in item 81, important factual data is inter-
     larded with fictitious dialogue.

     2. References to Falla in Monographs

93. Aguilar, Paco. "Un día de Manuel de Falla." *En
     las orillas de la música*. Buenos Aires: Edito-
     rial Losada, 1944, pp. 9-17.

         A colorful account of a day in the idiosyn-
     cratic life of the composer. Falla responded
     to the author, a friend, with a request that he
     suppress the fictional contention that he (Falla)
     considered musical composition a purely intuitive
     art.

94. Buckle, Richard. *Diaghilev*. 1st American ed.
     New York: Atheneum, 1979. 616 pp.

         Provides extensive information about the
     Ballets Russes' Spanish tour and on Falla's deal-
     ings with Diaghilev and his troupe.

95. Carner, Mosco. *Puccini: a Critical Biography*.
     2nd ed. London: Duckworth, 1974, p. 193.

         Describes Falla's rejection of a Spanish
     libretto offered by Tito Ricordi (1911) who had
     previously tried to interest Puccini in setting
     it to music.

96. Casella, Alfredo. *Music in my Time*. Translated
     and edited by Spencer Norton. Norman: University
     of Oklahoma Press, 1955. 254 pp.

        Explains Falla's role in founding the So-
     ciété Independent de Musique in Paris (1909)
     and in founding the Sociedad Nacional de Música
     in Madrid (1915). Recalls his stay in the com-
     poser's home in January of 1930.

97. Chase, Gilbert. *The Music of Spain*. 2nd rev. ed.
     New York: Dover, 1959. 383 pp.

        A comprehensive historical survey of Spanish
     music. Numerous references to Falla in addition
     to a chapter dedicated to a discussion of his
     music. The supplementary chapter, which is not
     contained in the first edition (New York: W.W.
     Norton & Co., 1941 and *La música de España* (Bue-
     nos Aires: Hachette, 1943)), describes the com-
     poser's plans to undertake a project with an
     Argentine writer Enrique Larreta.

98. Claudel, Paul. *Correspondance Paul Claudel-Darius
     Milhaud*. Cahiers Paul Claudel, no 3. Paris:
     Gallimard, 1961. 368 pp.

        More than a hundred letters transcribed
     here refer to the Claudel-Milhaud opera *Chris-
     tophe Colomb*, a work whose history is intertwined
     with that of *Atlántida*. Three of these letters
     refer specifically to Falla and his cantata:
     Claudel to Milhaud, 4 November 1927 and 23 Janu-
     ary 1928; and Milhaud to Claudel, [December
     1928]. Many others refer to José María Sert,
     who intended to design the sets and costumes
     for both works.

99. Cobb, Carl. *Federico García Lorca*. New York:
     Twayne Publishers, Inc., 1967. 160 pp.

        Argues that the article by Falla on *cante
     jondo* inspired Lorca's essay on the same subject,

and furthermore, that *The Three-Cornered Hat* was something of a model for the poet's *La zapatera prodigiosa*.

100. Diego, Gerardo; Rodrigo, Joaquín; and Sopeña, Federico. *Diez años de música en España*. Madrid: Espasa Calpe, S.A., 1949. 192 pp.

  Discusses Falla's influence on Spanish composers of the next generation.

101. Fraser, Andrew A. "Manuel de Falla." *Essays on Music*. London: Oxford University Press, 1930, pp. 56-65.

  A biographical sketch praising the extreme care that Falla took with his compositions. A response to criticisms of the paucity of his musical output.

102. García, Juan Alfonso. *Valentín Ruiz-Aznar (1902-1972): semblanza biográfica, estudio estético, y catálogo cronológico*. Granada: Real Academia de Bellas Artes, 1982. 147 pp.

  A history of Falla's personal and professional relationship with Ruiz-Aznar (organist and choir director at the cathedral), who in 1941 took charge of the papers that Falla had left behind in Granada. Quotes extensively from letters of Manuel and Germán de Falla.

103. García Lorca, Francisco. *Federico y su mundo*. 2nd ed. Edited and with a preface by Mario Hernández. Madrid: Alianza Editorial, 1981. 520 pp.

  A substantial chapter on Falla (pp. 148-57) in addition to many significant references elsewhere. Brings to light the nature and extent of the collaboration between the author's brother and the composer.

104. Gibson, Ian. *El asesinato de García Lorca*. Re-
      vised ed. Barcelona: Bruguera, 1981. 233 pp.

          Greatly revised and expanded version of
          The Death of Lorca (Chicago: J. Philip O'Hara,
          1973). Depicts Granada at the onset of the
          Civil War. Important background for anyone
          interested in the effect of the Nationalist
          takeover on the Spanish artistic community.

105. Hernández, Mario, ed. Introduction to *Primeras
      canciones, Seis poemas sueltos, Canciones po-
      pulares* by Federico García Lorca. Obras de
      Federico García Lorca, no. 5. Madrid: Alianza,
      1981. pp. 11-47.

          Argues that Falla and the "Instituto Libra
          de Enseñanza" were Lorca's most important teach-
          ers.

106. ————, ed.   Introduction to *Romancero gitano* by
      Federico García Lorca. Obras de Federico García
      Lorca, no. 1. Madrid: Alianza, 1981. pp. 7-
      46.

          Refers to Lorca's first trip to Seville
          (Holy Week 1921) in the company of his brother,
          Francisco, and Falla.

107. ————, ed.   Introduction to *Yerma* by Federico
      García Lorca. Obras de Federico García Lorca,
      no. 2. Madrid: Alianza, 1981. pp. 9-30.

          Quotes an article by Alardo Prats, *El sol*
          (Madrid), 15 January 1934, in which Lorca is
          interviewed. The young poet pays tribute to
          Falla who, in his words, is "a saint as well
          as a great artist."

108. Jackson, Gabriel. *La república española y la
      guerra civil*. 2nd ed. Translated by Enrique
      de Obregón. Barcelona: Editorial Crítica, 1976.
      496 pp.

The fundamental study. Describes the political roles of several of Falla's friends on both sides of the conflict, including José María Pemán and Fernando de los Rios.

109. Jiménez, Juan Ramón. *Cartas, primera selección.* Edited by Francisco Garfias. Madrid: Aguilar, 1962. 464 pp.

    Includes three letters in which the poet refers to Falla.

110. Landowska, Wanda. *Landowska on Music.* Collected, edited, and translated by Denise Restout with Robert Hawkins. New York: Stein & Day, 1964. 434 pp.

    Expounds on Falla's contributions to the revival of the harpsichord in the 20th century. Landowska recalls playing through parts of *El retablo de Maese Pedro* in Granada (1922) before it was completed.

111. Madariaga, Salvador. *Españoles de mi tiempo.* Barcelona: 1974. 468 pp.

    One of Spain's foremost essayists recalls his experiences with Falla and his music. Among several interesting anecdotes is the story of the composer's confrontation with an orchestra member who was not careful because he didn't think that his mistakes would be noticed. "God hears them all!" Falla responded. With drawings by Picasso and photographs.

112. Martínez, Julia. *Falla, Granados y Albéniz.* Madrid: Publicaciones Españolas, 1952. 30 pp.

    A brief biographical sketch of each of these composers.

113. Martínez Sierra, María. *Gregorio y yo: medio siglo de colaboración.* Mexico, D.F.: Biografías Gandesa, 1953. 312 pp.

Recalls several incidents from the year 1915, in which Falla travelled with the theater troop of the Martínez Sierras. His eccentricities are exaggerated, no doubt because of their parting of the ways.

114.   Menarini, Piero, ed. *Lola la comedianta* by Federico García Lorca. Preface by Gerardo Diego. Madrid: Alianza Editorial, 1981. 215 pp.

Transcribes and reproduces in facsimile the libretto written for Falla. The preliminary study describes the composer's role in this collaboration, and two letters from Lorca to Falla are reproduced in the preface, itself an important discussion of their personal and artistic relationship.

115.   Milhaud, Darius. *Notes Without Music*. New York: Knopf, 1953. 355 pp.

Milhaud presents his side of the story of his conflict with Falla over the similarity of their respective *Christophe Colomb* and *Atlántida*. Recalls his visit to Granada in 1929 and the subsequent sojourn that Manuel and María del Carmen de Falla made to Aix.

116.   Orenstein, Arbie. *Ravel, Man and Musician*. New York: Columbia University Press, 1975. 290 pp.

Refers to Ravel's trip to Granada in November of 1928 and to an unpublished letter received by Falla in March of 1930 in which Ravel discusses his strange project named after an airplane, "Dédale 39."

117.   Pedrell, Felipe. *Cancionero musical popular español*, 3rd ed., in 3 vols. Barcelona: Casa Editorial de Música, 1958. 151, 288, 233 pp.

Falla's principal source for the tradi-

tional melodies that he arranged and incorporated into several of his works. Annotated
copies of both the 1st edition (Valls: E.
Castells, 1918-22) and 2nd edition (Valls:
E. Castells, 1936) may be found among his books
in the family archives.

118. Pérez de Ayala, Ramón. "Manuel de Falla." *Amis-
      tades y recuerdos*. Edited by J. García
      Mercadel. Barcelona: Editorial Aedos, 1961.
      pp. 83-85.

           Excerpt from his article "Los cármenes de
      Granada," *ABC* (Madrid), 2 January 1955. His
      characterization of Falla's saintliness is often
      quoted.

119. Rodrigo, Antonio. *Lorca-Dalí: Una amistad tra-
      icionada*. Barcelona: Editorial Planeta, 1981.
      253 pp.

           Numerous references to Falla. Quotes from
      Falla-Lorca correspondence.

120. Salazar, Adolfo. *La música actual en Europa y
      sus problemas*. Madrid: J.M. Yagües, 1935.
      480 pp.

           Presents a Spanish view of contemporary
      music. Among the many isolated references to
      Falla is the description of his meeting with
      Stravinsky in Madrid in March of 1924.

121. —————. *Music in Our Time: Trends in Music Since
      the Romantic Era*. Translated by Isabel Pope.
      New York: Norton, 1946. 367 pp.

           Compares the folk idiom of Bartók, Falla,
      and Stravinsky.

122.   Samazeuilh, Gustave. "Manuel de Falla." *Musi-
       ciens de mon temps*. Paris: Éditions Marcel
       Daubin, 1947. pp. 334-40, 419-27.

            A biographical chapter and a list of piano
       arrangements of Falla's works.

123.   Seroff, Victor. *Maurice Ravel*. New York: Henry
       Holt & Co., 1953. 310 pp.

            Several interesting references to Falla.
       Describes a film project for which Delannoy,
       Falla, Ibert, Milhaud, and Ravel were asked to
       compose music for Chaliapin in the role of Don
       Quijote.

124.   Slonimsky, Nicolas. *Music Since 1900*. 4th ed.
       New York: Charles Scribner's Sons, 1971.
       1595 pp.

            Eighteen entries provide information about
       performances of Falla's works. The appendix
       contains the *Motu Propio* of Pope Pius X, which
       greatly influenced Falla's attitudes on sacred
       music.

125.   Stanton, Edward F. *The Tragic Myth: Lorca and
       Cante Jondo*. Lexington: University Press of
       Kentucky, 1978. 139 pp.

            Discusses Falla's role in initiating Lorca
       into the mysteries of *cante jondo*.

126.   Stravinsky, Igor, and Craft, Robert. *Memories
       and Commentaries*. London: Faber and Faber,
       1960. 183 pp.

            Contains a letter from Falla (22 August
       1929) lamenting the death of their common friend
       Serge Diaghilev. In his "portrait mémoire" of
       Falla, Stravinsky states that he has never met
       anyone as shy or unpityingly religious.

127. Stravinsky, Vera, and Craft, Robert. *Stravinsky in Pictures and Documents*. New York: Simon and Schuster, 1978. 688 pp.

      Describes the arrival of the Ballets Russes in Spain (May 1916). Contains an excellent group photograph featuring Diaghilev, Falla, and Stravinsky, as well as an excerpt of a letter from Falla dated 7 July 1916.

128. Subirá, José. "Lo novísimo y lo renovador en el siglo XX." *Historia de la música*, 2 vols., 2nd ed. Barcelona: Salvat, 1951. 2:615-88.

      Singles out Falla as the leader of Spain's musical renaissance. Suggests that if his early *zarzuelas* had been well-received, he might have become a great *zarzuela* composer like Federico Chueca (1846-1908) rather than an internationally known figure.

129. Trend, John Brand. "Music in the Gardens of Granada." *A Picture of Modern Spain: Men and Music*. London: Constable & Co., Ltd., 1921. pp. 237-45.

      Important account of the brief period in which Falla was living in Villa Carmona in Granada (1920).

130. Turina, Joaquín. *Escritos de Joaquín Turina*. Compiled and with notes by Antonio Iglesias. Madrid: Editorial Alpuerto, 1982. 238 pp.

      Contains several references to Falla, especially in the lecture, "Desenvolvimiento de la música española en estos últimos tiempos (pp. 215-23)" in which the significance of *La vida breve* is discussed. Reproduces Falla's piano reduction of the "Intermedio sinfónico" from this opera.

131.   Valls, Manuel. *La música española después de*
        Manuel de Falla. Madrid: Revista de Occidente,
        1962. 314 pp.

        A survey of the principal Spanish composers
        and their accomplishments since 1946. Derides
        the insular attitude prevalent in Spain, arguing
        that contemporary composers have yet to produce
        a work of greater interest than Falla's post-
        humous *Atlántida.*

3. Articles

132.   Alberti, Rafael. "En Alta Gracia con don Manuel
        de Falla." *La nación* (Buenos Aires), 16 Septem-
        ber 1945. Arts & Letters, p. 1.

        The author describes a poetry reading ac-
        companied with lute and piano which he gave in
        the home of Falla, who was too ill to attend a
        public performance of the same in the provincial
        capital of Córdoba.

133.   Altermann, J.P. "Manuel de Falla." *La revue*
        musicale 2 (June 1921): 202-16.

        Apotheosizes Falla and his works. Includes
        an engraved portrait by Larianow which is rarely
        reproduced.

134.   Aubry, Jean. "Manuel de Falla." *Musical Times,*
        1 April 1917. pp. 151-54.

        One of the earliest substantive biographies
        of Falla.

135.   ———. "Manuel de Falla." *Revista musical*
        hispano-americana, 30 April 1917, pp. 1-5.

        Translation of item 134.

136. Auric, Georges. "Manuel de Falla à l'Opéra Comique." *Les annales,* 15 April 1928, p. 366.

    This composer-critic praises Falla's *La vida breve, El amor brujo,* and *El retablo de Maese Pedro* at the expense of Marcel Delannoy's *Le marchand de lunettes,* which succeeded these works at the Opéra-Comique.

137. Bal y Gay, Jesús. "Manuel de Falla." *Nuestra música* 2 (January 1947): 19-24.

    Draws a parallel between the influence of Rubén Darío on the 20th-century poets of Spain and that of Debussy on Falla and his contemporaries. Argues that Falla, more than anyone else, was able to transcend the conservative adherence to nationalism.

138. Bramanti Jaúrequi, Enrique. "Entrevista con el médico de Falla, Ferrer Moratel." *La razón* (Buenos Aires), 11 January 1948, p. 3.

    Revealing glimpse into the final years of seclusion in Alta Gracia. Confirms other reports of Falla's extreme superstition.

139. Chase, Gilbert. "Manuel de Falla." *The International Cyclopedia of Music and Musicians,* 10th edition. Edited by Bruce Bohle. New York: Dodd, Mead, & Co., 1975. pp. 666-69.

    A clear, concise essay which was corrected by Falla himself (see item 303). Includes a catalog of works, transcriptions, and arrangements.

140. Chueca Goitia, Fernando. "Granada y el pintor Manuel Ángeles Ortiz." *ABC* (Madrid), 17 May 1962, p. 3.

    Describes the activities of the discussion group (*tertulia*) in which Falla, Lorca, and the painter, Ángeles Ortiz, participated: "El rinconcillo del café Alameda."

141. Diego, Gerardo. "Falla en tierra española." *La nación* (Buenos Aires), 2 February 1947, p. 5.

     Argues that the foundation of Falla's art was his interest in the great Spanish creators and creations: Scarlatti, Góngora, Cervantes, and the medieval romances and epics.

142. ———. "Falla y la literatura." *Ínsula* 13 (January 1947): 2-3.

     Reviews Falla's preferences in French and Spanish poetry. The composer himself is said to have written bilingual couplets to amuse his friends in Paris.

143. ———. "Turina." *ABC* (Madrid), 18 January 1949. p. 3.

     Reminisces about the time when Albéniz, Falla, and Turina were in Paris (1907-14).

144. D'Onofrio Botana, Reynaldo. "El secreto del arte de Falla." *El argentino* (La Plata), 22-23 December 1939. p. 1.

     Summarizes a lecture in Falla's honor presented by Ramón García de la Serna in the Verdi Library of La Plata, Argentina on 14 December 1939. Recalls a pilgrimage made to the home of the French poet, Théophile Gautier, by Falla, Lorca, and Serna.

145. "El Instituto de España." *ABC* (Seville), 12 January 1938. p. 3.

     Announces the reorganization of the former Royal Academies into a Spanish Institute. Falla refused to serve as its president despite great political pressure.

146. "El poema de la guerra." *ABC* (Seville), 7 October 1937. p. 1.

    A propagandistic article which exploits Falla's name and reputation by falsely claiming that he was overjoyed to have the opportunity to compose a war march for Franco.

147. "Falla, con los 'facciosos'!" *Ideal* (Granada), 2 November 1937, p. 1.

    Exemplary of the propagandistic articles written during the Civil War in which important figures like Falla were exploited as alleged adherents to Franco's movement. This particular piece appears to have been written in response to rumors that the composer was sympathetic to the Republican cause. See Falla's response in item 329.

148. Fernández-Cid, Antonio. "Falla, visto por Pemán." *ABC* (Madrid), 15 October 1960, p. 7.

    An interview with Franco's official poet, José María Pemán, who helped the invalid Falla during the years of civil war. Describes a trip they took to the Atlantic island of Sancti Petri which served as inspiration for *Atlántida*.

149. Franco, Enrique. "Doña María y sus músicos." *Arriba* (Madrid), 14 July 1981. p. 38.

    Tribute to the recently deceased playwright, María Martínez Sierra, whose collaborators included Falla, Turina, and the Basque composer Usandizaga (1887-1915).

150. ————. "Dos proyectos goyescos de Manuel de Falla." *El país* (Madrid), 7 May 1978. p. 12.

    Describes two offers of texts made to Falla, who wanted to join in commemorating the centenary of Goya's death (1927). The more

interesting of these is a mise-en-scène for a
movie about Goya by Luis Buñuel.

151.   ————. "El día que Falla se fue de Granada."
El país (Madrid), 23 July 1978. p. 10.

Quotes from the diary of Hermenegildo Lanz,
who designed the puppets for the Paris premiere
of *El retablo*. According to this account Falla
was disheartened by the brutality of the Civil
War and did not expect to return to Spain.

152.   ————. "Falla, Manuel de." *New Grove Dictionary
of Music and Musicians*. Edited by Stanley
Sadie. London: Macmillan, 1980. 6:371-74.

A surprisingly brief article. The extensive bibliography and work list are riddled
with factual errors. For example, the edition
of Falla's correspondence given as having been
published in 1976 was a projected work of the
author (Franco) that has not even been begun.

153.   ————. "Falla y los pajaritos de Unamuno."
El país (Madrid), 10 October 1976. p. 8.

Alludes to the fate suffered by Falla and
Unamuno, who were victimized by the Republicans
and the Nationalists during the Civil War, because they were liberals on the one hand and
devout Catholics on the other. Includes a
photograph of the paper birds that Unamuno made
for Falla.

154.   García, Juan Alfonso. "Manuel de Falla y la música eclesiástica." *Tesoro sacro musical*, no.
4, 1976, pp. 1-15; no. 3, 1977, pp. 10-23;
no. 4, 1977, pp. 1-13.

A lengthy, well-documented study. Quotes
extensively from unpublished correspondence in
an attempt to clarify the nature of Falla's
relationship with Eduardo Torres and Valentín

Ruiz Aznar, choir director and organist at the Seville cathedral, and José María Thomas, priest and choir director in Palma de Mallorca.

155. Grunfeld, Frederick. "Manuel de Falla and the 'Lost Continent.'" *High Fidelity/Stereo Review* 8 (January 1962): 39-44.

A colorful biographical sketch which focuses on the years of *Atlántida*'s composition. Recounts Falla's superstitious dread of a passing black limousine whose horn played Beethoven's Fate motif.

156. Istel, Edgar. "Manuel de Falla." *Musical Quarterly* 12 (October 1926): 497-525.

Provides a synopsis of *La vida breve*, *The Three-Cornered Hat*, and *El retablo de Maese Pedro*, as well as musical analyses of these works. Reproduces an autograph copy of a few measures from the *Retablo* dated January 1926.

157. "La epidemia de cólera del año 1885." *Diario de Cádiz*, 3 October 1976. pp. 8-9.

Describes the cholera epidemic that swept Cadiz when Falla was six years old. As a result he developed a lifelong fear of contamination.

158. Malherbe, Henri. "Chronique musicale: Manuel de Falla." *Feuilleton du Temps*, 14 March 1928, p. 1; 21 March 1928, p. 1.

A thorough discussion of Falla's music. Divides his ouevre into three style periods: nationalistic (1905-14); universal (1915-21), and neo-classic (1922-28).

159. Mayer Serra, Otto. "Falla's Musical Nationalism." *Musical Quarterly* 29 (January 1943): 1-17.

Divides Falla's oeuvre into a "19th century" nationalistic period and a "20th century"
neo-classic period. Analyzes *El retablo de
Maese Pedro* in great detail.

160. Millard Rosenburg, S.L. "Spanish Book-Letter."
      Modern Language Forum 18 (1 April 1933): 110-
      19.

Surveys the contemporary music scene in
Spain. Points out the influence of Falla on
the Mexican essayist, Alfonso Reyes, whom he
introduced to the *saetas* sung in Seville during
Holy Week.

161. Moragas, Rafael. "Ayer después de depositar
      flores en las tumbas de Isaac Albéniz y Jacinto
      Verdaguer." *La noche* (Barcelona), 25 March
      1927, p. 6.

A fascinating account of Falla's tribute
to these artists, as well as to Granados, who
was one of the unfortunate passengers aboard
the *Lusitania* when it was sunk by German tor-
pedoes. On this eleventh anniversary of his
death, Falla put an autograph passage from his
puppet play and a prayer in a bottle and threw
it into the Mediterranean.

*   ————. "Vida musical." *La noche* (Barcelona),
       21 June 1926. p. 8.

Cited below as item 196.

162. Odriozola, Antonio. "Las obras escénicas de
      Manuel de Falla." *ABC* (Madrid), 22 September
      1961, pp. 4-5.

Contains extensive data about important
performances.

163. Rodríguez Fernández, José. "Fechas memorables
      de la vida artística de Falla en Cádiz." *Diario
      de Cádiz*, 11 December 1926, p. 1.

          A brief biographical sketch. Contains
      valuable information on Falla's youth.

164. Rubinstein, Mauri. "Confidencias sobre la vida
      de Manuel de Falla." *Tic-tac* (Buenos Aires),
      15 December 1940, p. 7.

          An intimate account of the Fallas' day to
      day existence in Carlos Paz, Argentina.

165. Sagardia, Ángel. "Recuerdos y notas de estrenos
      de obras líricas españolas." *Radio nacional*
      (Madrid), 30 May 1943, pp. 1-2; 3 June 1943,
      pp. 1-2; 11 July 1943, p. 1.

          A series of articles dealing respectively
      with *La vida breve*, *El amor brujo*, and *El co-
      rregidor y la molinera*.

166. Sainz de la Maza, Regino. "Manuel de Falla en
      Buenos Aires." *Hispania* (Buenos Aires), 1939,
      pp. 20-22.

          Describes the evolution of Falla's oeuvre
      as a process of spiritual growth.

167. Sainz-León, Higinio. "Una hermana de Falla vive
      en Jerez de la Frontera." *Blanco y negro* (Ma-
      drid), 25 November 1961, pp. 3-4.

          A rare interview with María del Carmen de
      Falla, who reminisces about the years she lived
      with her brother in Cadiz, Granada, and Argen-
      tina.

168. Salazar, Adolfo. "Sociedad Nacional: Debussy,
      Ravel, Grieg." *El sol* (Madrid), 23 April 1920,
      p. 4.

Describes a performance of Debussy's Trio for harp, flute, and viola, with the harp part transcribed for piano and played by Falla.

169. ———. "Un maestro de la música moderna en la península." *La prensa* (New York), 23 August 1919, p. 3.

Early biography focuses on Falla's latest work *El corregidor y la molinera* and its transformation into *The Three-Cornered Hat*.

170. Samazeuilh, R.C. "A Day in Granada." *Chesterian*, December 1938, pp. 108-11.

The author describes his recent visit to Falla. Relates the composer's concern about rumors being circulated throughout Europe that he was losing his mind.

171. ———. "Falla Festival at San Sebastian." *Chesterian* 20 (November-December 1938): 50-52.

Reviews the performances held in the Kursaal of San Sebastian on 7 September 1938. Quotes from a letter Falla sent explaining that he was not feeling well enough to attend this festival.

172. Sanjuan, Pedro. "Música nueva: Manuel de Falla." *Diario de la marina* (Havana), 29 September 1927, p. 34.

The author, with a definite bias against Austria and Germany, describes the music of the 20th century as being controlled by the triumvirate: Falla, Ravel, and Stravinsky.

173. Segura, Florencio. "Un viaje con don Manuel." *Reseña*, November 1976, pp. 38-40.

A delightful travelogue. The car trip through Western Europe made by Andrés Segovia,

Falla, and his amanuensis, José Segura (the author's father) is reconstructed using the excerpts of Segura's letters to his wife.

174. Segura, Manuel. "Semblanza religiosa de Manuel de Falla." *Razón y fe*, July–August 1976, pp. 87–99.

An honest and well-documented study of Falla's religious beliefs and practices. Includes excerpts from private correspondence as well as public declarations made to newspaper editors.

175. Thomas, Juan María. "Manuel de Falla on the Island." *Chesterian* 22 (January 1948): 53–56.

Includes several vignettes from the author's monograph (item 90). Describes Falla's method of condensing *Parsifal* as much as possible so as to better understand it.

176. Trend, John Brand. "Falla in 'Arabia.'" *Music and Letters* 3 (April 1922): 133–49.

Demonstrates with musical examples the influence of the guitar on Spanish music, from Scarlatti to Falla. Discusses Falla's family in unusually great detail.

177. ———. "Recollections of Falla." *Musical Times*, January 1947, pp. 15–16.

Describes three meetings: their first in autumn of 1919, again in Holy Week of 1922, and the last encounter in 1932, when Falla played excerpts from *Atlántida* on the piano.

178. ———. "Two Books on Falla." *Chesterian* 22 (July 1948): 8–10.

Briefly mentions Thomas's *En la isla* (item 90) and Pahissa's *Vida y obra* (item 80). Of

more interest is the author's first-hand account
of Falla's religious and political beliefs.

179. Turina, Joaquín. "Manuel de Falla." *Chesterian*,
      n.s., no. 7 (May 1920): 193-96.

          Insightful discussion of Falla's composi-
      tional style. The libretto of *La vida breve*,
      Turina believes, suffered from changes made
      between the time of its composition (1905) and
      first performance (1913). Recalls conducting
      only seventeen musicians at the premiere of *El
      corregidor y la molinera*.

180. Vuillermoz, Emille. "Hommage à Falla." *Excelsior*
      (Paris), 16 May 1927, pp. 4-5.

          Notes that the gradual change in Falla's
      physical appearance coincides with the evolution
      of his music toward a more delicate and ethereal
      style.

181. Wirth, Helmut. "de Falla, Manuel." *Die Musik
      in Geschichte und Gegenwart*. Edited by
      Friedrich Blume. Kasel: Bärenreiter, 1949-.
      3:1747-57.

          Points out apparent contradiction in
      Falla's devotion to Spanish folk music, on the
      one hand, and to Chopin, on the other. Includes
      several photographs and a sample of his musical
      hand. Work list is accurate.

CHAPTER IV

SPECIALIZED STUDIES

1. *Music for Puppet-Plays, Ballets, and the Spoken Theater*

182. Aubry, Jean. "De Falla Talks of His New Work Based on a Don Quixote Theme." *Christian Science Monitor*, 1 September 1923, p. 17.

> Falla describes his literary preparation for *El retablo de Maese Pedro*.

183. ———. "*El retablo* by Manuel de Falla." *Chesterian*, n.s., no. 34 (October 1923): 37-46.

> Retells the story in detail and provides a scene-by-scene musical-dramatical analysis.

184. Beardsley, Theodore. "Manuel de Falla's Score for Calderon's *Gran teatro del mundo:* the Autograph Manuscript." *Kentucky Romance Quarterly* 16 (1969): 63-74.

> Provides a description and historical background of this seven-page autograph score.

* Benedito, Rafael. "Hablando con Manuel de Falla." *La patria* (Madrid), 15 April 1915, p. 3.

> Cited below as item 314.

185. Budwig, Andrew. "The Evolution of Manuel de
      Falla's *The Three-Cornered Hat* (1916-1920)."
      Journal of Musicological Research 5 (Spring
      1984): 191-212.

            Describes the transformation of the panto-
      mime *El corregidor y la molinera* into this bal-
      let, the most significant product of the Ballets
      Russes' wartime exile in Spain. Compares music
      and scenario of the pantomime and ballet ver-
      sions and quotes extensively from the unpub-
      lished correspondence of Falla, Diaghilev, and
      Gregorio Martínez Sierra.

186. "El corregidor y la molinera." *El noticiero uni-
      versal* (Barcelona), 4 July 1917, p. 8.

            Reveals that Diaghilev was interested in
      transforming this melodrama into a ballet *before*
      this performance in Barcelona took place. In
      this audience was the artist José María Sert,
      who later collaborated with Falla on the cantata
      Atlántida.

187. Escudero, Vicente. *Mi baile.* Barcelona: Montaner
      y Simón, S.A., 1947. 128 pp.

            Acclaims the incorporation of flamenco
      elements in *El amor brujo*, adducing a letter
      from Falla on this subject. Limited edition
      (1100 copies) includes many elegant drawings
      by the author in black, white, and tan.

*   ————. Letter to Remo Bufano, 4 March 1926.
      Boston Public Library.

            Cited below as item 300.

188. Falla, Manuel de. *The Three-Cornered Hat.* En-
      glish prose version by Robert Lawrence. New
      York: Random House, 1940. 40 pp.

            Designed to acquaint the general reader

with this ballet. Includes color illustrations after Picasso's original set and costumes and musical examples. Authorized by the Ballets Russes.

189. Franco, Enrique. "Historia de ballet: la 'farruca' de Félix el loco." *El país* (Madrid), 17 September 1978, Arte y Pensamiento, p. ix.

Relates the history of the gypsy dancer, Félix, who joined the Ballets Russes in their tour of Spain (1918-19) and taught Massine the *farruca*, which he incorporated in "The Miller's Dance" of *The Three-Cornered Hat*.

*   García Lorca, Francisco. *Federico y su mundo*. 2nd ed. Edited and with a preface by Mario Hernández. Madrid: Alianza Editorial, 1981. 520 pp.

Cited above as item 103.

190. ———. "La niña que riega la albahaca." *El país* (Madrid), 24 December 1977, Arte y Pensamiento, p. v.

Reconstructs this lost puppet play for which Falla provided the musical accompaniment (see item 103).

*   García Matos, Manuel. "Folklore en Falla." *Música* (Madrid) nos. 3-4, 1953: 41-68, no. 6, 1953: 33-52.

Cited below as item 270.

191. García Morillo, Roberto. "A veinteicinco años del *Tricornio*." *La nación* (Buenos Aires), 23 July 1944, p. 13.

A significant comparison of *El corregidor y la molinera* and *The Three-Cornered Hat*.

192. Lima, Robert. *The Theatre of García Lorca.* New
      York: Las Americas Publishing Co., 1963.
      338 pp.

          Provides details of the puppet performances
      produced by Falla and Lorca in the poet's home
      on 6 January 1923.

193. Massa, Pedro. "La Casona-Palacio de Larreta será
      museo de arte español." *ABC* (Seville), 5 May
      1962, p. 4.

          Explains why the collaboration between
      Falla and Enrique Larreta, who wanted to adapt
      his novel *La gloria de don Ramiro* for the thea-
      ter, was unsuccessful.

194. Massine, Leonide. *My Life in Ballet.* Edited by
      Phyllis Hartrell and Robert Rubens. London:
      Macmillan & Co., 1968. 318 pp.

          Relates his experiences as choreographer
      and dancer with Serge Diaghilev's Ballets Russes
      during that company's wartime exile in Spain
      (1916-19). Falla figures prominently in this
      account, for he and the Russians had a close
      relationship that ultimately gave birth to the
      splendid ballet, *The Three-Cornered Hat.*

*   Mayer Serra, Otto. "Falla's Musical Nationalism."
      Musical Quarterly 29 (January 1943): 1-17.

          Cited above as item 159.

*   Menarini, Piero, ed. *Lola la comedianta* by
      Federico García Lorca. Preface by Gerardo
      Diego. Madrid: Alianza Editorial, 1981.
      215 pp.

          Cited above as item 114.

195. Mora Guarnido, José. *Federico García Lorca y su mundo*. Buenos Aires: Losada, 1958. 239 pp.

Declarations about the nature of Falla's relationship with Lorca and the Martínez Sierras are based on unpublished correspondence. Argues that Falla left Spain with repugnance rather than fear of the regime.

196. Moragas, Rafael. "Vida musical." *La noche* (Barcelona), 21 June 1926, p. 8.

Notes the success of *El retablo de Maese Pedro* throughout the world and its recent triumph at the ISCM Congress in Zurich. Provides a brief history of its composition as well.

197. Paribeni, G.C. "Le prima alla Scala." *L'ambrosiano* (Milan), 31 January 1934, pp. 3-4.

Recounts the stories of *The Three-Cornered Hat* and *La vida breve* and analyzes the latter in terms of its role as a *verismo* opera.

198. Prunières, Henri. "De Falla Festival in Paris." *New York Times*, 8 April 1928, sec. 8, p. 9.

Explains the landmark significance of commemorative performances of *La vida breve*, *El amor brujo*, and *El retablo de Maese Pedro* which took place at the Opéra-Comique, and of the *Concerto* and *Siete Canciónes*, which were performed at the Salle Pleyel.

199. Ramírez, Ángel. "El corregidor y la molinera." *Música* (Madrid), 15 April 1917, pp. 2-3.

Reviews this premiere, conducted by Joaquín Turina, and proclaims it a great success.

200. Rivas Cherif, Cipriano de. "El tricorno." *España* (Paris), 28 February 1920, p. 2.

> A surprisingly unfavorable review of the London premiere. Provides an index of important names, including the dancers, artists, etc.

201. Salaverria, José. "Entrevista con Enrique Larreta." *ABC* (Madrid), 26 October 1920, p. 6.

> This Argentine novelist reveals his plans to collaborate with Falla and the artist, Ignacio Zuloaga.

202. Salazar, Adolfo. "El corregidor y la molinera." *Revista musical hispano-americano* (Madrid), 30 April 1917, pp. 8-12.

> Relates musical motifs to dramatic events in a convincing manner.

203. ————. "*El sombrero de tres picos* de Manuel de Falla, y la crítica francesa." *El sol* (Madrid), 4 June 1920, pp. 4-5.

> Counters French criticism that the Russians were merely aping traditional Spanish dances. Provides details of the Ballets Russes' tour of Spain.

204. ————. "Estreno de *El retablo de Maese Pedro* de Manuel de Falla." *El sol* (Madrid), 28 March 1924, p. 6.

> Points out folk melodies incorporated by Falla in this work.

205. ————. "Las obras de Falla en la Opéra-Comique y la crítica francesa." *El sol* (Madrid), 4 August 1928, p. 5.

> Summarizes the French press reviews of recent performances of *La vida breve*, *El amor*

brujo, and *El retablo de Maese Pedro* at the
Opéra-Comique.

206. ————. "Polichinela y Maese Pedro." *Revista
de Occidente* (Madrid), May 1924, pp. 229-37.

Compares these neo-classic works of Falla
and Stravinsky.

* ————. "Un maestro de la música moderna en la
península." *La prensa* (New York), 23 August
1919, p. 3.

Cited above as item 169.

207. Schwerke, Irving. "High Lights of the Zurich
Festival." *Musical Digest,* 13 July 1926, p. 7.

Acclaims *El retablo de Maese Pedro* as the
greatest success of the ISCM Festival.

208. Senior, Mary. "Introducing Ueber-Marionettes."
New York Sun, 10 December 1925, sec. 2, p. 1.

Describes in detail the puppets used for
the performance of *El retablo de Maese Pedro*
sponsored by the League of Composers. Reproduces the instructions Falla sent to the directors of this society (see item 303).

2. Opera

209. Amestoy, Santos. "Entrevista con López Cobos."
Pueblo literario (Madrid), 29 December 1976,
p. 12.

Points out the contradictory behavior of
Ernesto Halffter, who declared (on 9 September
1976) the Lucerne version of *Atlántida* the "definitive" one, but then began speaking (on 23
September 1976) of a new "complete" version
which would receive its premiere in Spain.

210. Ansermet, Ernest. "Falla's *Atlántida*." *Opera News*, 29 September 1962, pp. 8-13.

> Refers to a symphonic poem dedicated to the city of Seville which Falla intended to compose after he completed his concerto. Provides an insightful musical-dramatical analysis of *Atlántida* which includes musical examples.

211. Antoine, Rainer. "Berlin Bouquet." *Opera News*, 8 December 1962, p. 30.

> Describes in detail G.R. Schelner's fanciful German adaptation of *Atlántida* done for the Berlin Deutches Oper.

212. Barce, Ramón. "*Atlántida*, el problema formal." *La estafeta literaria* no. 258 (Madrid), 2 February 1963, pp. 14-15.

> Argues that although the proportions of Falla's *Atlántida* and Verdaguer's *L'Atlàntida* are different, their narrative structure is similar.

213. Boas, Robert. "Lucerne Festival." *Music and Musicians*, December 1976, p. 64.

> Appraises revised version of *Atlántida*. Advocates an outdoor performance in a public square, as was done for the *auto sacramentales* of the 17th century.

214. Bucher, Felix. "*Atlántida* von Manuel de Falla." *Vaterland* (Lucerne), 18 August 1976, p. 3.

> Enumerates the mythological and historical references in *Atlántida*. Refers to the letter from Falla to his set designer, José María Sert, dated 10 November 1928, which contains an early draft of the libretto.

*   Budwig, Andrew. "Manuel de Falla's *Atlántida*: an Historical and Analytical Study." Ph.D. Dissertation, University of Chicago, 1984. 474 pp.

        Cited above as item 59.

215. ————. "Una metodología para el estudio de la *Atlántida* de Manuel de Falla." *La revista de musicología* 4 (June 1982): 150-56.

        Provides an introduction to the sources available for the study of *Atlántida* and suggests methods of working with this material. Traces the origins of the Greek acclamation at the beginning of Part 2 and of the Greek music quoted by Falla in his autographs.

216. Casella, Alfredo. "Visita a Manuel de Falla." *L'Italia litteraria*, 2 February 1930, pp. 3-4.

        Written by Casella immediately upon his return from Granada. States that Falla had yet to decide whether his *Atlántida* would be a staged or purely musical work.

217. Chase, Gilbert. "Falla's Epic *Atlántida*." *Stereo Review* 41 (August 1978): 130-31.

        Reviews the recording made by the Spanish National Orchestra and Chorus under Rafael Frühbeck de Burgos. Includes a brief history of the work and a discussion of the problems posed by its completion.

*   Chiesa, Hector. "La música española--dice Manuel de Falla--es parte de un arte imperecedero." *El pueblo* (Buenos Aires), 19 October 1939, p. 3.

        Cited below as item 315.

*   Claudel, Paul. *Correspondance Paul Claudel-*
       Darius Milhaud. Cahiers Paul Claudel, no. 3.
       Paris: Gallimard, 1961. 368 pp.

       Cited above as item 98.

*   "Corrientes." *Nueva época* (Buenos Aires), 23
       October 1939, p. 7.

       Cited below as item 316.

218.   d'Amico, F. "Italy, a Revival and a Premiere."
       Musical America 82 (September 1962): 102.

       Reviews the Scala premiere of *Atlántida*
       and traces its origins back to the German ora-
       torio.

219.   Delgado Carrero, José. "El Cordobés será Colón
       en la *Atlántida* de Dalí." *Pueblo* (Madrid), 31
       July 1965, p. 10.

       Salvador Dalí claims that he is working
       on a production of *Atlántida* in which the bull-
       fighter "El Cordobés" will play Columbus. In-
       cludes a photograph of the two.

220.   Diego, Gerardo. "Poesía de la *Atlántida*." *ABC*
       (Seville), 29 November 1962, pp. 11-13.

       Draws parallels between the use of mytho-
       logical reference in *Atlántida* and its use in
       classic (17th-century) Spanish poetry.

221.   ⸺. "Un momento de la *Atlántida*." *ABC*
       (Seville), 28 November 1962, p. 6.

       Examines the tribute to Cadiz--"Era teu
       front, oh Gades"--contained in Falla's *Atlán-*
       tida.

222. Fernández-Cid, Antonio. "Manuel de Falla y la *Atlántida*." *ABC* (Madrid), 14 November 1956, pp. 3-4.

Describes the contents of *Atlántida* as related to the author by Ernesto Halffter, who anticipates completing the work in summer of 1957.

223. ————. "Sobre la *Atlántida*." *ABC* (Madrid), 29 January 1958, p. 8.

Compares the problems that Falla had composing *Atlántida* with those that Ernesto Halffter is having completing it.

224. Fernández Shaw, Guillermo. *Larga historia de "La vida breve": años de lucha de Manuel de Falla*. Madrid: Impreso de los Talleres Gráficos de la Sociedad General de Autores Españoles, 1964. 32 pp.

The author vindicates his father's libretto in this brief compositional history of the opera.

225. ————. *Larga historia de "La vida breve."* Madrid: Ediciones de la Revista de Occidente, 1972. 214 pp.

A greatly expanded version of item 224 Includes the complete text of the opera and excerpts from the correspondence of Falla and Fernández Shaw. Refers to two projects proposed by the composer: *A buen juez mejor testigo* (after Zorilla) with Fernández Shaw and *Tragedia de una noche de verano* with the Martínez Sierras.

226. Franco, Enrique. "En torno a *La vida breve*." *Música en España* (Madrid), December 1980, pp. 21-23.

Provides new details about *La vida breve*, which, the author argues, has an antecedent in *La tempranica* of the *zarzuela* composer Gerónimo Giménez (1854-1923).

227. ————. "España ante la *Atlántida*." *Arriba* (Madrid), 25 June 1954, pp. 11-12.

Interviews Ernesto Halffter, who reveals his plans for completing *Atlántida* and overseeing its performance.

228. ————. "Estreno de una obra inédita de Manuel de Falla." *El país* (Madrid), 23 June 1976, p. 10.

Reviews the premiere of a symphonic adaptation of the unfinished opera *Fuego fatuo* (see item 36). Agrees with Pahissa (cf. item 80) that Falla abandoned this project as a result of lack of interest on the part of impresarios, and not because he was worried about the moral implications of the libretto, as María Martínez Sierra suggests (cf. item 113).

229. ————. "La *Atlántida* no tiene misterio." *Arriba* (Madrid), 18 October 1960, p. 6.

A response to a wave of articles in the Spanish press demanding that the truth about *Atlántida* be made known to the public. Quotes (1) a letter from Ernest Ansermet dated January 1959 declaring that Falla nearly completed the cantata, and (2) a letter from Falla to the editors of *El sol* dated 21 November 1931 (see item 317).

230. ————. "La grande avventura di *Atlántida*." *Musica d'oggi* 5 (July 1962): 4-5.

The only article on *Atlántida* authorized by Falla's heirs. Provides a multitude of details about the contracts signed with Ricordi and the manner in which the autographs were turned over to the publisher. Rationalizes Ernesto Halffter's addition of a Finale by suggesting that Falla may have considered doing the same.

231. ———. "Por fin *Atlántida*." *El país* (Madrid), 15 May 1977, p. 8.

Restates the often-asked questions concerning Falla's intentions for the performance of *Atlántida*. The title alludes to the fact that Spain has been waiting for a definitive version of the work for over thirty years.

232. ———. "Spain." *Musical Quarterly* 48 (1962): 248-51.

Provides general background on the content of *Atlántida* and the history of its performance in Spain.

233. Gara, Eugenio. "Nella riemersa *Atlántida* l'angelo meridiano di Manuel de Falla." *Musica d'oggi* 5 (July 1962): 91-93.

A favorable review of the Scala premiere of *Atlántida*, with photographs of eight scenes from Parts 2 and 3. Compares this cantata to Stravinsky's *Oedipus Rex*.

*   García Matos, Manuel. "Folklore en Falla." *Música* (Madrid) nos. 3-4, 1953: 41-68; no. 6, 1953: 33-52.

Cited below as item 270.

234. Gisbert Padró, Juan. "Origen de *Atlántida*." *ABC* (Madrid), 29 December 1960, pp. 3-4.

The author explains his role in interesting Falla in Jacint Verdaguer's *L'Atlántida*. A significant revelation, it unfortunately lacks documentary evidence.

235. Goebel, W.F. "Eine Nachgelassene de Falla-Oper
      in Mailand." *Oesterreichische* 17 (August 1962):
      385-90.

           Calls the Scala premiere of *Atlántida* a
      "monumental monstrosity." Attacks the composi-
      tion itself, as well as this production, sug-
      gesting that it will never appeal to the public
      in the way that Falla's ballets have.

*   Grunfeld, Frederick. "Manuel de Falla and the
      'Lost Continent.'" *High Fidelity/Stereo Review*
      8 (January 1962): 39-44.

           Cited above as item 155.

236. Guerrero Martin, José. "Ernesto Halffter: por
      los caminos de Falla." *La vanguardia* (Barce-
      lona), 19 October 1980, Weekend sec., pp. 8-9.

           Interviews Ernesto Halffter, who candidly
      admits that after having studied the *Atlántida*
      autographs for the first time, he thought that
      he could complete the cantata in three months.
      Provides an inside view of the political machi-
      nations which surrounded the arrangements for
      its premiere in Spain.

237. Guillén, Julio D. "De este libro sacó Manuel de
      Falla el libreto para la *Atlántida*." *El alcázar*
      (Madrid), 16 January 1961, p. 4.

           Interviews Ernesto Halffter, who mistakenly
      claims that he possesses Falla's working copy
      of Jacint Verdaguer's *L'Atlántida*. This copy,
      given to him by Germán de Falla, contains sig-
      nificantly fewer notations of Manuel de Falla
      than two others housed in the family archives
      (see item 59).

238. Halffter, Cristóbal. "*Atlántida*: el tratamiento
      coral." *La estafeta literaria*, no. 258 (Ma-
      drid), 2 February 1963, pp. 30-31.

Argues that the four-part Protestant chorale is the principal precursor of the choral writing in Falla's cantata rather than Spanish Renaissance polyphony as has elsewhere been suggested.

*   Hall, Raymond. "An Interview with Manuel de Falla." *New York Times*, 23 November 1930, sec. 8, p. 8.

Cited below as item 330.

239. Heyworth, P. "Falla's *Atlántida*." *New York Times*, 10 December 1961, sec. 2, p. 17.

An unfavorable review of the concert premiere of *Atlántida*. Describes the lengthy dispute between Ricordi and the Spanish government over the right to the first performance.

240. Ibarrola, Alonso. "Pronto se estrenará en la 'Scala' de Milán, con decorados de Picasso." *Diario de Cádiz*, 22 August 1960, p. 2.

Propagates the rumor that Picasso had agreed to design the costumes and set for the Scala premiere of *Atlántida*.

241. Iglesias, Antonio. "Falla's Posthumous *Atlántida* to Be Premiered at Cadiz in 1956." *Musical America*, 1 January 1955, p. 34.

Reviews Ernesto Halffter's progress and describes the plans being made for the trimillenary celebration of the founding of Cadiz. Reveals that Falla's heirs had originally wanted to publish the *Atlántida* autographs in facsimile.

242. Knepler, G. "Argentine *Atlántida*." *Opera News*, 28 September 1963, p. 27.

Reviews the first Catalan language performance of the complete *Atlántida*.

243. "La *Atlántida* de Manuel de Falla." *El sol*, 12
      November 1931, p. 4.

          An inaccurate description of this work in
      progress based on the report of an undisclosed
      "friend of the composer." Falla responded
      quickly in a letter to the editor of this news-
      paper (see item 317).

244. Lang, Paul Henry. "Philharmonic Hall-Opening
      Festival Ends." *New York Herald Tribune*, 1
      October 1962, p. 14.

          Points out the lack of unity in the version
      of *Atlántida* conducted by Ernest Ansermet.
      Stresses the need for a scholarly examination
      of the autograph score so that the world will
      know what Falla intended.

245. Lonchampt, Jacques. "Fallait-il terminer *L'At-
      lantide* de Falla?" *Le monde*, 16 December 1961,
      p. 11.

          Raises doubts about the authenticity of
      the first version of *Atlántida*, performed in
      Barcelona in November of 1961. Repeats criti-
      cism of Falla's friend and biographer Roland
      Manuel, who rejects the orchestral passage in
      the number "Les Caravelles" as uncharacteristic.

246. Machlis, Joseph. "Notes on the Program." Intro-
      duction and translation of *Atlántida* by Manuel
      de Falla. *Opening Week at Philharmonic Hall*.
      New York: Metropolitan Opera, 1962, pp. 39-56.

          Includes a short biographical sketch, a
      résumé of the story, and the text of the English
      translation by Joseph Machlis used in this per-
      formance of the Prologue, Part 1, and most of
      Part 3 of *Atlántida*.

247. Massa, Pedro. "Verdaguer, Falla, la *Atlántida*."
     La prensa (Buenos Aires), 18 January 1942, p. 4.

     Draws parallels between the lives of the
     poet and the composer.

248. Mila, Massimo. "Valori dell' *Atlántida*." *Musica
     d'oggi* 5 (July 1962): 171-78.

     Reviews the Scala premiere. Includes pho-
     tographs of four scenes from this production
     as well as musical examples and a facsimile of
     folio A19 of the autograph score.

*   Milhaud, Darius. *Notes Without Music*. New York:
     Knopf, 1953. 355 pp.

     Cited above as item 115.

249. Montale, Eugenio. "Il mito di *Atlántida*."
     Corriere d'informazione, 21-22 May 1962, p. 6.

     A favorable review of the Scala premiere
     by the Nobel laureate who prepared the Italian
     translation. Discusses the literary origins
     of *Atlántida* and provides a history of its com-
     pletion.

250. Oehlmann, W. "Mythos, Revue, und Oper, Gustav
     Rudolf Sellner inszenierte de Falla-Halffters
     Atlántida in der Bismarkstrasse." *Neue Zeit-
     schrift für Musik* 123 (December 1962): 553-54.

     An unfavorable review of the Berlin pre-
     mière, includes a photograph from the opening
     scene. Raises doubts about the significance
     of *Atlántida* with respect to other works by
     Falla.

*   Paribeni, G.C. "Le prima alla Scala."
     L'ambrosiano (Milan), 31 January 1934, pp. 3-4.

     Cited above as item 197.

251.   Pedrell, Felipe. "La vida breve." *La vanguardia* (Barcelona), 29 May 1913, p. 2.

A touching review by Falla's friend and teacher. Quotes from correspondence exchanged at the time of the opera's completion. Argues that Falla had to go to Paris to gain recognition because he did not have the sort of personality which would enable him to sell himself in Madrid.

252.   Querol, Miguel. "La *Atlántida* de Falla y su estreno." *ABC* (Seville), 12 March 1958, p. 55.

Presents evidence that Falla wanted the premiere of *Atlántida* in Barcelona. Quotes from a letter he wrote to the city government shortly before his death (see item 306).

253.   Salas Viu, Vicente. "The Mystery of Manuel de Falla's *Atlántida*." *Inter-American Music Bulletin* 33 (January 1963): 1-6.

Provides a detailed history of *Atlántida*, in English, from its conception in 1926 to its completion by Ernesto Halffter in 1962. Apparently derived from the article by Franco (item 230) authorized by the Falla family.

*   Salazar, Adolfo. "Las obras de Falla en la Opéra-Comique y la crítica francesa." *El sol* (Madrid), 4 August 1928, p. 5.

Cited above as item 205.

254.   Sartori, Claudio. "*Atlántida* reaches the stage." *Opera* 13 (September 1962): 599-601.

A favorable review of the Scala premiere which nevertheless criticizes the work's excessive length. Includes a photograph of Teresa Stratas as Queen Isabella.

255.   Schonberg, Harold C. "Met Gives *Atlántida* Pre-
        mière." *New York Times*, 1 October 1962, sec.
        8, p. 1.

            Provides detailed information about this
        unique U.S. performance. Like Lang (see item
        244) the author deplores the lack of a schol-
        arly study.

256.   Sopeña Ibáñez, Federico. *"Atlántida"*: intro-
        ducción a Manuel de Falla. Madrid: Taurus,
        1962. 100 pp.

            A history of *Atlántida* with a strong po-
        litical bias. Falla's cantata is analysed in
        terms of its religious and nationalistic sig-
        nificance only. The Appendix is most useful
        as it contains several letters from Falla to
        Ángel Barrios, a friend in Granada, and to the
        British scholar John Trend, as well as other
        sources for the study of *Atlántida*.

257.   Starkie, Walter. *"Atlántida."* *Saturday Review*,
        11 November 1961, pp. 64-65.

            Recalls his visits to Falla in 1921, 1928-
        30, and the summer of 1935. During this final
        visit, the composer played excerpts from *Atlán-
        tida* and expressed his admiration for the music
        of Grieg.

258.   Stuckenschmidt, H.H. "Berlin (West)." *Opera* 13
        (December 1962): 803-5.

            Describes the changes made in Falla's story
        for the Berlin performance of *Atlántida*. Con-
        cludes that this production, like the musical
        reviews of the 1920's was overdone.

259.   Valls, Manuel. "*Atlántida*, la cantata sin fin."
        Destino, no. 1774 (Barcelona), 2 October 1971,
        pp. 17-20.

        Argues that Falla was prevented from com-
        pleting his cantata by uncertainties of esthetic
        intent.

260.   Vian, Cesco. "Il poeta de *L'Atlantide*: Manuel
        de Falla." *L'Italia* (Rome), 21 December 1961,
        p. 5.

        A thorough discussion of Falla's adaptation
        of the Catalan epic *L'Atlàntida*. Explains how
        verse forms in this language differ from those
        in Italian and Castilian.

    3. *Falla as Folklorist: Piano Music, Songs,*
        and the "Concurso del Cante Jondo"

261.   Bilbao Aristegui, Pablo. "Dos temas populares
        vascos en la obra de Falla." *Estudios vizcainos*
        3 (January-June 1971): 173-77.

        Argues convincingly that Falla incorporated
        two Basque melodies in the Movement "Pedrelli-
        ana" from the orchestral suite *Homenajes*.

262.   Chase, Gilbert. "Manuel de Falla's Music for
        Piano Solo." *Chesterian* 21 (January-March
        1940): 41-46.

        Takes issue with the then-prevalent prac-
        tice of performing piano transcriptions of
        Falla's orchestral works--and especially the
        "Ritual Fire Dance" from *El amor brujo*--while
        ignoring the pieces he composed for piano.

263.   Crichton, Ronald. "Falla-Berio." *Financial*
        Times, 17 March 1978, p. 8.

        Describes the arrangement of Falla's *Seven*
        Songs dedicated to Cathy Berberian by Luciano

Berio. The instrumental ensemble employed is said to be very similar to that of *El amor brujo.*

264. Diego, Gerardo. "Crónica del Centenario de Góngora (1627-1927)." *Informaciones* (Madrid), 26 May 1977, Artes y Pensamientos, pp. 5-7.

Provides important historical background for the study of Falla's "Soneto a Córdoba" after Góngora. The composer's low opinion of this poet's ouevre is said to have been changed by Lorca.

265. ———. "Las canciones de Falla." *La nación* (Buenos Aires), 15 December 1945, pp. 5, 8.

Essentially the same as item 266.

266. ———. "Las canciones de Falla." *Música* 12 (1 June 1945), pp. 14-15.

A thorough literary and musical analysis of all of Falla's songs, including the almost-forgotten *Trois mélodies* after Gautier.

267. Falla, Manuel de. *El "cante jondo" (canto primitivo andaluz).* Granada: Editorial Urania, 1922. 23 pp.

The seminal essay on the subject, it kindled the interest of composers, collectors of folk music, and poets. Lorca's essay, "Importancia histórica y artística del primitivo canto andaluz llamado Cante Jondo" (reprinted in item 75), is little more than a paraphrase of this study. Reprinted by Molina Fajardo (item 75), in a collection of Falla's essays (item 285), and in Italian by Mila (item 347).

268.   ————. "La proposición del cante jondo." *El de-*
        fensor de Granada, 21 March 1922, p. 2.

        The composer's reply to the criticism of
        a few musicians and journalists who believed
        that the "Concurso de Cante Jondo" proposed by
        Falla and his friends was a waste of the city's
        funds. Reprinted in item 75.

269.   Franco, Enrique. "Las canciones inéditas." *El*
        país (Madrid), 28 November 1976, p. 11.

        Lays the foundation for a study of Falla's
        unpublished songs. Includes a brief history
        of the composer's musical education.

270.   García Matos, Manuel. "Folklore en Falla." *Mú-*
        sica (Madrid) nos. 3-4, 1953: 41-68; no. 6,
        1953: 33-52.

        Looks for folk melodies in *La vida breve,*
        Noches en los jardines de España, The Three-
        Cornered Hat and *El retablo de Maese Pedro.*
        An interesting view of Falla's work, though
        the findings are not always convincing.

271.   Iglesias, Antonio. *Manuel de Falla: su obra para*
        piano. Madrid: Editorial Alpuerto, 1983.
        328 pp.

        Analyzes all of Falla's piano works. Dis-
        cussions of rhythm and repetition are valuable
        but fail to discuss tonality, dynamics, articu-
        lation, etc. Includes many musical examples
        and reproduces title pages of out-of-print edi-
        tions.

272.   Legendre, Maurice. "La Fête-Dieu à Granade en
        1922." *Le correspondant,* 10 July 1922, pp.
        148-55.

        Describes his impressions of Falla's home
        and the "Concurso del Cante Jondo." Recognizes

the importance of preserving folk music so that
it may serve as a basis for "universal" (art)
music.

273. Pemán, José M. "Canto de marcha para los soldades
españoles." *Obras completas*, 7 vols. Madrid:
Escelicier, S.L., 1947, 1:1124.

This poem was commissioned by the Nationalists and presented to Falla for a musical
setting (see item 54).

4. *Orchestral and Chamber Music*

274. Ager, Laurence. "*Fanfare*." *Musical Times* 108
(November 1967): 1001-2.

A brief history of the publication, *Fanfare*
(1921-22), whose first issue contained Falla's
"Fanfare pour une fête," reproduced here.

275. Aubry, Jean. "Manuel de Falla's *Psyché*." *Christian Science Monitor*, 19 September 1925, p. 19.

A discussion of this little-known chamber
work by the author of its poetic text.

276. Diego, Gerardo. "Los *Homenajes* de Falla." *ABC*
(Madrid), 14 November 1947, pp. 6-7.

Gives the history of each of the four hom-
mages and of their transformation into an orchestral suite (1936-39).

277. Gullón, Ricardo. *Relaciones amistosas y lite-
rarias entre Juan Ramón Jiménez y los Martínez
Sierra*. San Juan: Ediciónes de la Torre, 1961.
138 pp.

Discusses the influence of the Martínez
Sierras on Falla. His *Noches en los jardines
de España* is said to have been inspired by their
essay, *Granada (Guia emocional)*.

*   Istel, Edgar. "Manuel de Falla." *Musical Quar-
      terly* 12 (October 1926): 497-525.

          Cited above as item 156.

278. Moragas, Rafael. "Anoche el triunfo que alcanzó
      en el Liceo Manuel de Falla." *La noche* (Barce-
      lona), 18 March 1927, p. 7.

          Acclaims the performance of Frank Marshall
      in Falla's *Noches en los jardines de España*.
      Quotes a statement made by the composer on this
      interpretation and the work in general.

279. Thomas, Juan María. "Manuel de Falla's Concerto."
      Chesterian 8 (December 1926): 92-93.

          Criticizes concert of 5 November 1926 in
      which *Noches en los jardines de España* was per-
      formed by Falla and the Casals orchestra, and
      the world premiere of the *Concerto* included
      Wanda Landowska at the harpsichord.

280. Villar, Rogelio. "Falla y su *Concierto de
      cámera*." Lecture presented at the Teatro María
      Guerrero, 21 December 1931. Madrid: Publica-
      ciones de *Ritmo*, 1932. 16 pp.

          A eulogistic rather than analytic discus-
      sion. Describes Falla as a "stylizer of popular
      elements."

CHAPTER V

PRIMARY SOURCES FOR FALLA RESEARCH

1. Essays on Music and Musicians

281.   ————. "Claude Debussy et Espagne." *La revue musicale*, special no. (December 1920): 206-10.

Reprinted as "Claude Debussy and Spain," *Chesterian* n.s., no. 12 (January 1921). This tribute opens with the quip: "Claude Debussy has written Spanish music without ever having gone to Spain." Falla admired this ability—which he himself lacked—to evoke exotic settings without having experienced them first hand.

282.   Falla, Manuel de. "¿Cómo son la nueva juventud española?" *La gaceta literaria* (Madrid), 1 February 1929, p. 1.

This fascinating discourse has surprisingly never been reprinted. In it, Falla candidly expresses his opinions on the nature of the compositional process, on the course that Spanish music is taking, and on the government's failure to lend music sufficient support.

*   ————. *El "cante jondo" (canto primitivo anda-luz)*. Granada: Editorial Urania, 1922. 23 pp.

Cited above as item 267.

283. ———. "El gran músico de nuestro tiempo: Igor Stravinsky." *La tribuna* (Madrid), 5 June 1916, p. 4.

   Praises Stravinsky as an innovator and calls for more performances of his music in Spain.

284. ———. "Enrique Granados, evocación de su obra." *Revista musical hispano-americana* (Madrid), 30 April 1916, pp. 11-12.

   A brief tribute to his colleague, who had recently died on the *Lusitania*.

285. ———. *Escritos sobre música y músicos.* 3rd ed. Introduction and notes by Federico Sopeña. Madrid: Espasa-Calpe, 1972. 162 pp.

   A slightly expanded version of the first (Comisión General de la Música, 1947) and second (Espasa Calpe Argentina, 1950) editions. Reprints items 267-68, 281, 283-84, 286, 288-91, and 324. Introductory prefaces by the editor are more poetic than informative.

286. ———. "Felipe Pedrell." *La revue musicale* 4 (February 1923): 1-11.

   A lengthy tribute to Pedrell as the teacher of Albéniz, Granados, and Falla himself. Enumerates his accomplishments both as a composer and a musicologist.

287. ———. "Homenaje a Debussy." *El universo* (Madrid), 28 April 1918, p. 2.

   The text of the homage read by Falla in the Ateneo of Madrid on 27 April 1917 (Artur Rubenstein played the Spanish premiere of Debussy's "Soirée dans Grenade"). Under the influence of wartime jingoism Falla describes Debussy as "a Latin--one of us--of that great and invincible race."

288. ————. "Introducción a la música nueva." *Revista musical hispano-americana* (Madrid), December 1916, pp. 4-6.

In the first part, Falla denounces the malevolent and ignorant critics, who are always inimical to new music, and also those who accept contemporary music undiscerningly as an improvement on that of the past. The accomplishments of the 20th century masters are summarized in the second part: the creation of new modes to replace major-minor tonality, the liberation from a reliance on thematic development, etc.

* ————. "La proposición del cante jondo." *El defensor de Granada*, 21 March 1922, p. 2.

Cited above as item 268.

289. ————. "Notas sobre Ricardo Wagner en el cincuentenario de su muerte." *Cruz y raya*, September 1933, pp. 30-37.

Criticizes Wagner as yet another megalomaniac in "that enormous carnival which we call the 19th century." Nevertheless, he lauds the innovations his compositions ushered in, especially *Parsifal*.

290. ————. "Notes sur Ravel." *La revue musicale* 20 (March 1939): 81-86.

Describes Ravel's art as well formed but delicate. Discusses a number of works which reveal the composer's Spanish heritage. Translated into French by Alexis Roland-Manuel. Original Spanish version first appeared in *Isla* (Jeréz de la Frontera), September 1939.

291. ————. "Nuestra música." *Música* (Madrid), 1 June 1917, pp. 1-5.

Praises the new generation of Spanish

composers whose music is inspired by that of
the *pueblo*. Criticizes the outdated *zarzuela*
with its exaggerated emphasis on major-minor
tonality.

292.   ————. *On Music and Musicians*. Introduced by
Federico Sopeña. Translated by David Urman
and J.M. Thorson. London: Marion Boyars, 1979.
117 pp.

A translation of item 285, with some ad-
ditional commentary by the translators.

*   ————. Prologue to *La música francesa contem-
poránea* by Jean Aubry. Unpublished. Reprinted
in *Revista musical hispano-americana* (Madrid),
July 1916, pp. 7-13.

Cited below as item 324.

293.   ————. *Spanien und die neue Musik: ein Lebens-
bild in Schriften, Bildern, Erinnerungen.*
Translated and edited by Jacoba Grunfeld. Zü-
rich: Verlag der Arche, 1968. 184 pp.

Includes all of Falla's major essays as
well as eleven of his letters to Isaac Albéniz,
Felipe Pedrell, Ricardo Viñes, and others. Extensive end material includes a chronology of
events, discography, catalogue of works, and a
bibliography with over a hundred and fifty en-
tries.

294.   ————. "Una autocrítica." *El país* (Madrid),
28 November 1976, Arte y Pensamiento, p. i.

The text of an unpublished essay that Falla
sent to the musicologist Cecilio de Roda. Analyzes his *Cuatro piezas españolas* for piano,
explaining how each evokes the ambience of the
region indicated in its title.

295. ──────. "Wanda Landowska à Grenade." *La revue musicale* 4 (February 1923): 73-74.

> A poetic account of Landowska's Granada performances.

2. *Correspondence*

296. Bustos, Juan. "La correspondencia entre Manuel de Falla y Joaquín Rodrigo." *Patria* (Granada), 7 January 1982, p. 8.

> Excerpts from this correspondence demonstrate Falla's persistence in helping Rodrigo obtain a study grant.

297. Dille, D., ed. [Falla-Bartók Correspondence.] *Documenta Bartokiana*, 4 vols. Mainz: B. Schotts Söhne, 1968, 3:158-60.

> Contains a transcription of a letter from Falla dated 22 February 1931 as well as a facsimile of the second half of this letter. Describes the tour of Spain that he had helped Bartók arrange.

298. Dukas, Paul. *Correspondance de Paul Dukas.* Edited by Georges Farie. Paris: Éditions Durand et Co., 1971. 199 pp.

> Contains two letters to Jacques Durand (a publisher of Dukas and Falla) which refer to Falla. The second, dated 18 July 1919, announces the imminent premiere of *The Three-Cornered Hat.*

299. Falla, Manuel de. *Cartas a Segismundo Romero.* Transcribed and edited by Pascual P. Recuero. Granada: Excmo. Ayuntamiento, Patronato Casa-Museo Manuel de Falla, 1976. 494 pp.

> Contains a transcription of the complete correspondence (128 pieces) from Falla to this

Sevillian cellist. Includes a well-documented
history of Falla's Granada years (1920-36) as
well as facsimiles of most of the cursive letters (over a hundred pages worth).

300. ———. Letter to Remo Bufano, 4 March 1926.
Boston Public Library.

An unpublished letter in which Falla reacts
to the very positive criticism *El retablo de
Maese Pedro* received after its United States
premiere. Includes a copy of Bufano's response.

*   ———. *Spanien und die neue Musik: ein Lebens-
bild in Schriften, Bildern, Erinnerungen.*
Translated and edited by Jacoba Grunfeld. Zurich: Verlag der Arche, 1968. 184 pp.

Cited above as item 293.

301. Fundación Juan March. "Epistolario Falla-
Rodrigo." *Homenaje a Joaquín Rodrigo.* Madrid:
Fundación Juan March, 1981. pp. 24-53.

Edition of thirty-five letters dated between 1928 and 1938. The anonymous editor
egregiously transcribes the name of Falla's
sister as Pilar (his brother's sister-in-law)
instead of María del Carmen.

*   Garcia, Juan Alfonso. *Valentín Ruiz-Aznar (1902-
1972): semblanza biográfica, estudio estético,
y catálogo cronológico.* Granada: Real Academia
de Bellas Artes, 1982. 147 pp.

Cited above as item 102.

302. García Lorca, Federico. *Cartas, postales, poemas
y dibujos.* Edited by Antonio Gallego Morell.
Madrid: Editorial Moneda y Crédito, 1968.
175 pp.

Transcribes ten letters to Falla, several

of which refer to their projected collaborations
on puppet plays and the operetta *Lola la comedianta*. Includes a striking color reproduction
of a harlequin portrait that Lorca included
with a letter to Falla dated August 1922.

303. Gilbert Chase Collection of Manuel de Falla's
      Correspondence (1931-1945). New York Public
      Library, Lincoln Center.

          Two dozen letters, many of which contain
      Falla's commentary and corrections of the proofs
      of Chase's biographical article (see item 139).

304. Hernández, Mario. "García Lorca y Manuel de
      Falla: una carta y una obra inédita." *El país*
      (Madrid), 24 December 1977, Arte y Pensamiento,
      p. iv.

          Contains a facsimile of a postcard (San
      Sebastian, 5 August 1923) in which Lorca de-
      scribes his ideas for *Lola la comedianta*.

305. Jiménez, Juan Ramón. *Selección de cartas, 1899-
      1958*. Edited by Antonio Beneyto. Colección
      la esquina, no. 5. Barcelona: Ediciones Picazo,
      1973. 418 pp.

          Transcribes four letters to Falla dating
      from 1921 to 1935.

306. Junyent, Eduardo, and Riquer, Martín de, eds.
      [Manuel de Falla to Mayor of Barcelona, 6 July
      1945.] In Preface to *L'Atlàntida* by Jacint
      Verdaguer. Barcelona: Ayuntamiento de Barce-
      lona, 1946.

          In this letter Falla declines an invitation
      to stage *Atlántida* in Barcelona for the centen-
      ary celebration of Verdaguer's birth.

307. League of Composers Collection of Letters from
      Manuel de Falla to Mrs. Arthur M. Ries and

Mrs. Claire R. Ries (1925–30). New York Public Library, Lincoln Center.

One of the most important sources of information on the practical problems presented by Falla's puppet play. Includes five letters in which detailed instructions for mounting a performance of *El retablo de Maese Pedro* are provided.

308. [Manuel de Falla correspondence.] Mary Flagler Cary Music Collection, Pierpont Morgan Library.

Five letters dated 1927 to 1930. Includes two letters to Walter Damrosch declining invitation to New York because of his commitment to *Atlántida*.

309. "Manuel de Falla, el gran maestro español dirigirá un concierto en nuestra ciudad." *Hoy* (Buenos Aires), 17 May 1942.

Reproduces letter from Falla to Amadeo Ramírez (26 March 1942), in which the composer agrees to conduct part of a benefit concert.

* Menarini, Piero, ed. *Lola la comedianta* by Federico García Lorca. Preface by Gerardo Diego. Madrid: Alianza Editorial, 1981. 215 pp.

Cited above as item 114.

* Pahissa, Jaime. *Vida y obra de Manuel de Falla.* Buenos Aires: G. Ricordi & Co., 1947. 207 pp.

Cited above as item 80.

310. Pérez Gutiérrez, Mariano. *Falla y Turina: a través de su epistolario.* Madrid: Editorial Alpuerto, 1982. 159 pp.

Transcribes most of the extant Falla-Turina

correspondence. Of special significance is
the letter from Falla (25 June 1917) containing
corrections for the score of *El corregidor y
la molinera*, which Turina subsequently conducted
in Barcelona. The commentary, derived from
the standard biographies, is nonetheless enlivened with photographs, reproductions of programs, and excerpts from the correspondence
between Turina and his fiancée (both were inti-
mates of Falla during their years in Paris).

311. Poulenc, Francis. *Correspondance 1915-1963*. Edited by Hélène de Wendel. Paris: Éditions de
Seuil, 1967. 276 pp.

Contains four letters from Falla (1920-35).
The one dated 26 September 1929 is especially
significant for its discussion of the harpsichord, as Poulenc and Falla were the first composers in the 20th century to compose for that
instrument.

312. Ruiz Tarazona, Andrés. "La correspondencia Falla-
Olallo Morales." *Ritmo*, no. 467 (December
1976): 40-41.

Transcribes seven letters from Falla, who
encourages and advises the conductor Morales.
In a letter dated 31 May 1936, he makes the
final arrangements for a trip to Copenhagen
(Morales' home), which never materialized because of the Civil War that began in July.

* Sopeña Ibáñez, Federico. *"Atlántida": introducción a Manuel de Falla*. Madrid: Taurus,
1962. 100 pp.

Cited above as item 256.

313. ———, editor. *Correspondencia entre Falla y
Zuloaga, 1915-1942*. Granada: Ayuntamiento de
Granada, 1982. [63 pp.]

Transcribes all of Zuloaga's letters to
Falla and copies of Falla's letters to him that
are presently in the possession of the composer's heirs.

*   Stravinsky, Igor, and Craft, Robert. *Memories
and Commentaries*. London: Faber and Faber,
1960. 183 pp.

Cited above as item 126.

*   Thomas, Juan María. *Manuel de Falla en la isla*.
Palma de Mallorca: Ediciones Capella Clàssica,
1947. 341 pp.

Cited above as item 90.

3. *Declarations, Interviews, and Special
Musical Publications*

*   Aubry, Jean. "De Falla Talks of His New Work
Based on a Don Quixote Theme." *Christian Science Monitor*, 1 September 1923. p. 17.

Cited above as item 182.

314.   Benedito, Rafael. "Hablando con Manuel de Falla."
La patria (Madrid), 15 April 1915, p. 3.

Falla admits that only three months elapsed
from the day the dancer Pastora Imperio proposed
the idea of writing a gypsy ballet to the day
he and the Martínez Sierras completed *El amor
brujo*. States that he never wanted to be a
touring virtuoso and that originally he had
wanted to be a writer rather than a musician.

315.   Chiesa, Hector. "La música española--dice Manuel
de Falla--es parte de un arte imperecedero."
El pueblo (Buenos Aires), 19 October 1939, p. 3.

An interview with Falla, who laments the
state of his health, and as a consequence, the

extent of *Atlántida*'s incompletion. Compares
his life in Argentina and Spain.

316.   "Corrientes." *Nueva época* (Buenos Aires), 23
       October 1939, p. 7.

           Falla describes *Atlántida* as an *auto sac-
       ramental* or a *misterio* for chorus and orchestra.
       He declares that in spite of rumors to the con-
       trary, he will not return to Spain until the
       war ends and his health improves.

317.   Falla, Manuel de. "Carta de Falla." *El sol* (Ma-
       drid), 21 November 1931, p. 4.

           Responds to an inaccurate description of
       his *Atlántida* that appeared in *El sol* (see item
       243).

318.   ———. "Fanfare pour une fête." *Fanfare* 1 (Au-
       gust 1921): 10.

           This short-lived journal commissioned Falla
       to write a fanfare for its first issue (see
       items 39 and 274).

319.   ———. "Hommage 'Le tombeau de Claude Debussy.'"
       La revue musicale 1, musical supplement (Decem-
       ber 1920): unpaged.

           Falla's only work for guitar. Published
       alongside pieces by Bartók, Dukas, Ravel, Satie,
       and Stravinsky.

320.   ———. "La alta esperanza." *Patria* (Granada),
       4 May 1938.

           A declaration of Falla's support of the
       Nationalist regime. Judging from attitudes ex-
       pressed in his personal correspondence, this
       article is more propagandistic than factual.

321. ————. "Pour le tombeau de Paul Dukas." *La
revue musicale*, special no. (May-June 1936):
7-9.

> Includes other compositions in memory of
> Dukas by Messiaen, Rodrigo, and others.

322. ————. Preface to *Escuela razonada de la gui-
tarra*, by Emilio Pujol. Buenos Aires: G.
Ricordi & Co., 1954. p. i.

> Acclaims the harmonic richness of the gui-
> tar, whose sonorities are echoed in the music
> of Domenico Scarlatti, Glinka, Debussy, and
> Ravel.

323. ————. Prologue to *La enciclopedia abreviada
de música*, in 2 vols., by Joaquín Turina. Madrid: Renacimiento, 1917. pp. i-iv.

> After praising this scholarly work, Falla
> warns the reader that music cannot be considered
> an intellectual pastime as is, for example,
> the game of chess.

324. ————. Prologue to *música francesa contempo-
ránea* by Jean Aubry. Unpublished. Reprinted
in *Revista musical hispano-americana* (Madrid),
July 1916, pp. 7-13.

> Contends that Debussy did more than any
> other composer to restore the "pure" French
> musical tradition of Rameau and Couperin.
> Praises Aubry for undertaking this study and
> acknowledges the debt that he and other Spanish
> composers owe to France. Falla wrote this pro-
> logue for a Spanish translation of Aubry's *La
> musique française d'aujord'hui* (Paris: Perrin
> et Cie., 1916) that was subsequently abandoned.

325. ————. "Soneto a Córdoba." *Litoral* 5-7 (October
1927): 46-47.

Falla's contribution to this issue com-
memorating the tricentennial of Góngora's birth.
The autograph score of this song with harp accompaniment is reproduced in facsimile.

326. ———. "Una carta de don Manuel de Falla." *La
unión* (Seville), 10 June 1932, p. 5.

One of the few public declarations in which
Falla expresses his religious beliefs. He explains that it is impossible for him to accept
an hommage offered by the city of Seville when
God himself has been refused recognition by
the government. This criticism of Republican
anticlericalism sparked several responses in
liberal and conservative newspapers. Reprinted
in *Ideal* (Granada) 14 June 1932, p. 5.

327. ———. "Una carta." *Diario de Cádiz*, 3 July
1932, p. 2.

Falla's response to the acceptance (cf.
Debate [Madrid] 11-12 June 1932) and rejection
(cf. *La socialista* [Madrid] 14 June 1932) of
his belief that Spain must be a Catholic nation.

328. ———. "Una carta de Falla." *Diario de Cádiz*,
21 August 1934, p. 1.

Falla expresses his adherence to the hommage honoring Gerónimo Giménez (1854-1923), a
composer of *zarzuelas*. He suggests that either
the Teatro or the Plaza Manuel de Falla be re-
named after Giménez.

329. ———. "Una carta de Falla." *Ideal*, 5 November
1937, p. 1.

Falla's response to government propaganda
(see item 147). He affirms his political neu-
trality and expresses his belief that God will
solve Spain's crisis.

330.   Hall, Raymond. "An Interview with Manuel de
       Falla." *New York Times*, 23 November 1930, sec.
       8, p. 8.

              Conducted in Granada in October of 1930.
       Falla emphasizes the immensity of his concep-
       tion. Includes a synopsis of Verdaguer's
       L'Atlàntida, the poem upon which his cantata
       is based.

331.   Pereda, Patricio de. "La interviú que no quiso
       dar el maestro Falla." *Radio nacional* (Madrid),
       22 October 1939, p. 1.

              Approached in Tangiers on his way from
       Barcelona to Buenos Aires, Falla refused this
       interview, no doubt to prevent the government-
       controlled press from further exploiting him.

332.   Pino, Rosario. "Una información de *Mujer*." *Mujer*
       (Madrid), 6 January 1926, p. 2.

              Several prominent Spaniards are asked the
       questions: "What is life's greatest short-
       coming? Its greatest attraction?" Falla's
       answers are surprisingly cynical: "Inquietude.
       Nothing."

333.   Santiago, Iñigo de. "Manuel de Falla, desde la
       Argentina, habla para *Arriba*." *Arriba* (Madrid),
       8 October 1944, p. 4.

              Falla expresses his desire to return to
       Spain and live in a village in the province of
       Cordova. He also gives his opinion on some of
       the Spanish literature that he has recently
       read.

334.   Villar, Rogelio. "Músicos españoles: Manuel de
       Falla." *La ilustración española y americana*,
       15 June 1917, pp. 340-41.

              Falla talks about his own music and that
       of his contemporaries.

CHAPTER VI

TRIBUTES TO FALLA

1. *Collections of Essays, Special Journal
   Issues, and Literary Tributes*

335. Comisión Pro Monumento a Manuel de Falla. *El
     homenaje de Córdoba a Manuel de Falla*. Córdoba,
     Argentina: Comisión Pro Monumento a Manuel de
     Falla, 1956. 80 pp.

     Contains interesting photographs of the
     Argentine monuments dedicated to Falla as well
     as plans for upcoming inauguration of a monument
     carved by Vicente Torró Simó.

336. *Destino*, no. 1774 (Barcelona), 2 October 1971.
     48 pp.

     This special Falla issue includes articles
     by Rafael Abella, José Casanovas, Sebastián
     Gasch, Xavier Montsalvatge, Manuel Orozco, and
     Manuel Valls (see item 259).

337. Hernández, Mario, ed. Introduction to *Diván del
     Tamarit, Llanto por Sanchez Mejías, Canciones
     populares* by Federico García Lorca. Obras de
     Federico García Lorca, no. 3. Madrid: Alianza,
     1981. pp. 9-52.

     Contains the text of Lorca's "Soneto de
     homage a Manuel de Falla ofreciéndole unas
     flores" and important commentary.

338. *Ínsula* 13 (January 1947). 52 pp.

      This issue dedicated to Falla contains
      articles by Gerardo Diego (see item 142), Sopeña
      Ibáñez, and others.

339. Jiménez, Juan Ramón. "Manuel de Falla (1926)."
      Españoles de tres mundos (1914-40). Introduc-
      tion and edition by Ricardo Gullón. Madrid:
      Afrodisio Aguado, S.A., 1960, pp. 154-55.

      One of one hundred fifty biographical
      sketches of Spaniards from the New, Old, or
      Other World (see title). Originally published
      in Buenos Aires: Losada, 1942.

340. ————. *Olvidos de Granada, 1924-28*. Illustrated
      by Ángel Ferrant. San Juan: Editorial de la
      Torre, 1960. 73 pp.

      Includes two poems and two biographical
      sketches dedicated to Falla and his sister.
      "Manuel de Falla 2 (1926)" is the same as item
      339 above. Falla, Lorca, and Jiménez himself
      narrowly escape the evil spell cast on them by
      three gypsies in the semi-fictional "Las tres
      diosas brujas de la Vega." Beautifully illus-
      trated with watercolor washes.

341. Jofré García, Rafael, ed. *Manuel de Falla y Gra-
      nada*. Granada: Centro Artístico, Literario y
      Científico, 1963. [42 pp.]

      A tribute to Falla and Granada consisting
      of poems, character sketches, and photographs
      of the section of Granada where Falla lived.
      The letter from Falla to his puppet designer,
      H. Lanz, and a photograph that Stravinsky dedi-
      cated to Falla are especially interesting.

342. *La estafeta literaria*, no. 233 (Madrid), 22 February 1962. 77 pp.

This special issue, designated "Manuel de Falla desde *Atlántida*," contains brief articles by Ramón Barce, Manuel Cassa, Vicente Marerro, Lorenzo Riber, Fernando Ruiz Coca, and Federico Sopeña Ibáñez. Includes textual excerpts from two of the cantata's numbers: "Cantic à Barcelona" and "El somni d'Isabel."

343. *La estafeta literaria*, no. 258 (Madrid), 2 February 1963. 58 pp.

Another issue of this journal dedicated to *Atlántida* (see item 342). Contains two interesting analyses (see items 212 and 238) as well as several brief eulogies.

344. *La estafeta literaria*, nos. 592-93 (Madrid), 15 July/1 August 1976. 43 pp.

A special double issue designated "Centenario a Falla." Contains a significant bibliography (see item 382) as well as cursory articles by Carlos José Costas, Carlos Gómez Amat, Tomás Marco, and Joaquín Valverde Sepúlveda.

345. L'Institute Français en Espagne. "Hommage à Manuel de Falla." *Bulletin des bibliothèques de L'Institute Français en Espagne*, 13 December 1946. 19 pp.

Contains eulogies by José Cúbiles, Gerardo Diego, José Francés, Maurice Legendre, and Joaquín Turina. Closes with a bibliographical note and excerpts from two of Falla's essays (see items 281 and 286).

346. *Litoral*, nos. 35-36 (Malaga), January-February
      1973.   86 pp.

           This issue, entitled "De Cádiz a Granada,
      homenaje a Manuel de Falla," contains some very
      fine prose and poetry by Spain's most prominent
      authors. Juan Ramón Jiménez contributed a spir-
      itual and physical description of the composer,
      and Rafael Alberti wrote about his last meeting
      with Falla and about a projected collaboration
      (originally published in 1945; see item 132).

347. Mila, Massimo, ed. *Manuel de Falla: con saggi
      di Melchior de Almagro San Martin et al., e
      scritti di Manuel de Falla*. Translated by Mario
      Bartolotto et al. Milano: G. Ricordi & Co.,
      1962.   362 pp.

           A collection of articles and excerpts from
      monographs, in the original Italian or trans-
      lated. Among the more interesting pieces are
      those by Gilbert Chase and Enrique Franco (see
      items 97 and 230). Includes a bibliography
      and discography.

348. Ministerio de Educación Nacional. *Libro-programa
      de la primera audición mundial de* "Atlántida."
      Madrid: Ministerio de Educación Nacional, 1961.
      22 pp.

           Contains a reproduction of the parliamen-
      tary bill (11 September 1961) authorizing gov-
      ernment funding of this premiere, as well as
      articles by Antonio Blanco Freijeiro (on mythol-
      ogy), and biographies of Falla and Jacint
      Verdaguer, by Gerardo Diego and José María
      Castro Calvo.

349. Molina Fajardo, Eduardo. "Soneto de homenaje a
      Manuel de Falla." *La estafeta literaria*, 15
      November 1970, p. 5.

           Announces the discovery of a letter from

Lorca to Ramón Pérez de Roda containing two drawings and a sonnet honoring Falla (see items 337 and 352). Points out that Falla, Lorca, and their friends founded the Ateneo de Granada in 1927.

350. *Música*, no. 12, 1 June 1945. 49 pp.

The only collection of articles about Falla published during his lifetime. Among the contributors are Gerardo Diego, Adolfo Salazar, and Federico Sopeña Ibáñez.

351. *Musica d'oggi* 5 (July 1972). 178 pp.

This special *Atlántida* issue contains a number of significant articles including those cited above, by Franco (item 230), Gara (item 233), and Mila (item 248).

352. Orozco, Manuel. "Un soneto desconocido de Federico." *Litoral* 8-9 (September 1969): 17-20.

Announces the discovery of a sonnet by Lorca which praises Falla's efforts to preserve his native folk song. This is also the first discussion of their collaboration on the operetta *Lola la comedianta*.

353. Puig Claramunt, Alfonso. *Ballet y baile español*. Barcelona: Montaner y Simón, 1944. 199 pp.

A tribute to ballet in Spain with a good deal of emphasis on Falla and the Ballets Russes. Includes black and white plates depicting scenes from *El amor brujo* and *The Three-Cornered Hat*.

354. *Reseña*, no. 99, November 1976. 48 pp.

Includes a number of short, general articles. The only significant item is Florencio Segura's documented description of a tour of

Western Europe taken by his father, Falla, and Andrés Segovia (see item 173).

355.   *Ritmo*, no. 323, December 1961. 162 pp.

This special *Atlántida* issue includes a synopsis of Verdaguer's epic, *L'Atlàntida*, and four facsimiles of Falla's autograph score. Focuses on reporting the public and critical reaction to the premiere in Barcelona.

356.   *Ritmo*, no. 467, December 1976. 103 pp.

This special Falla issue opens with a marvelously illustrated biographical sketch by José Luis Garcia del Busto. It also contains a number of short articles, but more significant are facsimiles of autograph scores and letters and photographs (see item 366).

2. *Published Lectures and Articles*

357.   Alejandro, Luis. "Dolor y emoción de Tenerife ante el cadáver de Falla." *La tarde* (Tenerife), 9 January 1947, p. 1.

Includes a brief interview with María del Carmen de Falla, who states that her brother died of cardiac arrest rather than from his chronic stomach problems. She also discusses *Atlántida* and the state of her financial affairs.

358.   Ara, Pedro. *El espíritu de Manuel de Falla*. Lecture presented at the Colegio Militar de la Nación, 24 October 1950. Buenos Aires: Balmes, 1951. 37 pp.

A eulogistic address delivered by Falla's former physician, who immediately after his death, deposited all of the composer's scores, letters, and other important documents in a bank vault.

359. Castillo Puche, Luis. "En donde se cuenta cómo vivió Manuel de Falla sus últimos días en la Córdoba de Argentina." *Pueblo* (Madrid), 19 May 1959. pp. 2-3.

> Reconstructs Falla's daily routine in Alta Gracia, Argentina. Includes photographs of his home "Los espinillos."

360. Collet, Henri. "La mort de Manuel de Falla." *La revue musicale* 204 (January 1947): 27-28.

> Excerpts three letters from Falla (1914-28) in which his generosity and love for France are demonstrated.

361. "Entregan a Granada la partitura manuscrita de Manuel de Falla." *La prensa* (Lima), 14 November 1980, p. 2.

> Describes the presentation of the autograph score of *La vida breve* by the Director of Music and Theater from the Spanish Ministry of Culture. Colección Poesía. Madrid: Editora Nacional, 1970, pp. 93-96.

362. Franco, Enrique. "Clausura de curso en el Ateneo: Homenaje a Strawinsky y Falla." *Arriba* (Madrid), 25 May 1971, p. 15.

> A summary of the lecture presented by Federico Sopeña Ibáñez in which the religious views of the two composers are compared.

* ———. "Falla y los pajaritos de Unamuno." *El país* (Madrid), 10 October 1976, p. 8.

> Cited above as 153.

363. Halffter, Ernesto. "El magisterio permanente de Manuel de Falla." *Discurso de la Real Academia de Bellas Artes de San Fernando*. Madrid: Real Academia de San Fernando, 1973. 23 pp.

The lecture presented by Falla's former
student upon his admittance into the Royal Academy of Fine Arts, with a response by Federico
Sopeña Ibáñez. Platitudinous but useful insofar
as it provides an insight into Falla's relationship with Halffter.

364. ————. *Falla en el centenario de su nacimiento.*
Madrid: Ministerio de Educación y Ciencia, 1977.
82 pp.

Expands on the material presented in an
earlier lecture (see item 363). Provides new
details about his plans for the Spanish premiere
of the cantata's "definitive" version.

365. ————. *Falla en su centenario.* Madrid: Ministerio de Educación y Ciencia, 1977. 26 pp.

A condensed version of item 364.

366. "Iconocrafía Manuel de Falla." *Ritmo*, no. 467
(December 1976): 89-93.

Contains reproductions of all of the standard portraits: four drawings, three oil paint-
ings, and two busts.

367. Herrero Antolín, Antonio. *Biografía escolar de
Manuel de Falla.* Palencia: Caja de Ahorros y
Préstamos, 1976. 44 pp.

A tribute on the centenary of Falla's birth
written for elementary school students. Exem-
plifies the manner in which the "official" biography (in which Falla is portrayed as a zeal-
ous Catholic and patriot) formulated during
the years of Franco's regime continues to be
propagated.

*   Jiménez, Luis. *Mi recuerdo humano de Manuel de
Falla.* Presented at a conference of the Comisión Pro-Centenario de la Muerte de Manuel

de Falla, 28 April 1976. Granada: University of Granada, 1980. 79 pp.

Cited above as item 73.

368. Ortíz de Villajos, C.C. "Granada siente la ausencia de Falla." *El diario español* (Buenos Aires), 18 May 1944, p. 2.

Recalls an interview with Falla in 1929. The composer's friends prevailed upon the author not to publish anything about his personal eccentricities.

369. Salazar, Adolfo. "Manuel de Falla o el mar de por medio." *Ultramar* (Mexico, D.F.), 1947, p. 1.

A moving account of Falla's isolation during the Spanish Civil War.

370. Zuñiga, Edelmira. "La Casa-Museo de Manuel de Falla." *Mujeres* (Mexico, D.F.), 30 September 1978, pp. 48-49.

A portrait of "El carmen de Ave María," the house in Granada that Falla rented from 1921 to 1941. Also describes Falla's first residence in that city, "El carmen de Santa Engracia."

3. Catalogs, Anthologies, and Selected Recordings

371. Excmo. Ayuntamiento de Granada. *Centro Cultural "Manuel de Falla."* Granada: Excmo. Ayuntamiento de Granada, 1980. [12 pp.]

Outlines the history and function of this auditorium-library in both Spanish and English. Includes floor plans and photographs.

372. Falla, Manuel de. *Atlántida.* With Enriqueta Tarrés, Anna Ricci, Vicente Sardinero, Eduardo

Giménez, and Paloma Pérez Iñigo; and the National Orchestra and Chorus of Spain, cond.
Rafael Frühbeck de Burgos. Angel SBLX-3852.

Provides the original Catalan libretto
with an anonymous English translation. Articles
by Ernesto Halffter and Enrique Franco.

373. ————. *Fanfare pour une fête*. Leonard Bernstein
conducting the Orchestre National de France.
Columbia M35102.

The only commercial recording of this work.
The liner notes by Peter Eliot Stone provide
information on its premiere and publication.

374. ————. *Inéditos de Manuel de Falla*. Montserrat
Alavedia, soprano; Manuel Carra, piano; and
Pedro Gorostola, violoncello. RCA SRL-2466.

The only recording of Falla's student compositions. Liner notes are by Enrique Franco
who edited these works (see item 375).

375. ————. *Obras desconocidas*, in 3 vols. Edited
by Enrique Franco. Madrid: Unión Musical Española, 1980. 27, 15, 11 pp.

Volume 1 contains pieces for mezzo-soprano
and piano: "Preludios," "Olas Gigantes," "Dios
mio, que solo se quedan los muertos," "Oración
de las madres que tienen a sus hijos en brazos,"
and "Canción andaluza: El pan de ronda." Volume
2 contains pieces for violoncello and piano:
"Melodía" and "Romanza." Volume 3 contains
pieces for piano solo: "Canción," "Cortejo de
gnomos," and "Cante a los romeros de Volga"
(Song of the Volga Boatmen).

376. Franco, Enrique. *Exposición Manuel de Falla*.
Catalog for an exposition in the Antiguo Hospi-
tal de Santa Cruz. Madrid: Ministerio de Educación y Ciencia, 1976. [46 pp.]

Contains twenty black-and-white reproductions of autograph scores, letters, drawings, and photographs. Descriptions of the contents of the exhibition cases are cryptically brief.

377. ————. *Manuel de Falla en el centenario de su nacimiento (1876-1976)*. Catalog for an exposition in the Galeria de Exposiciones, Banco de Granada. Granada: Fundación Rodríguez-Acosta, 1976. 41 pp.

A catalog of one hundred eighty-five items, arranged chronologically. Includes two color photographs of Falla portraits and a facsimile of the "Oración de las madres que tienen sus niños en brazos."

378. Kastiyo, José Luis. *Casa-Museo "Manuel de Falla."* Obra cultural, no. 7. Granada: Caja de Ahorros de Granada, 1971. 14 pp.

A tribute to Falla presented in the form of a tour of his newly restored home. Includes large color photographs.

379. Orozco, Manuel. "La Casa de Manuel de Falla." *Casa-Museo de Manuel de Falla*. Preface by María Isabel de Falla with a biographical essay by Enrique Franco. Granada: Casa-Museo Manuel de Falla, 1980. pp. 7-31.

A clever arrangement of important information. Each of the pencil sketches made by Hermenegildo Lanz, who made a pictoral record of each room and the garden before it was dismantled in 1941, is displayed opposite a color photograph of the same scene in the newly restored house. Orozco transcribes the letter from Falla to his lawyer Borrajo (27 January 1941) in which he requests that his belongings be moved out of the house. Franco's essay is a reprint of item 69 above.

380.   Picasso, Pablo. *Designs for "The Three-Cornered Hat" (le Tricorne).* Edited by Parmenia Migel. New York: Dover Publications, Inc., 1978. 56 pp.

Reproduces all of the plates in item 381 as well as part of the contract between Serge Diaghilev and the Spanish dancer, Félix Fernández García. Includes a chronology, bibliography, and discography.

381.   ————. *Treinte-deux reproductions de maquettes en couleurs d'après les originaux de costumes et décor par Picasso pour le ballet "Le tricorne."* Paris: Paul Rosenberg, 1920.

A limited edition (250 copies) of color reproductions of Picasso's sketches for the set and costumes that he designed for the premiere of *The Three-Cornered Hat* in the Alhambra Theatre in London on 21 July 1919. 32 plates.

4.   *Bibliographies, Discographies, and Work Lists*

382.   Blas Vega, José. "Bibliografia de Manuel de Falla." *La estafeta literaria* (Madrid) 15 July-1 August 1976, pp. 15-17.

Over a hundred items, several of which are either fictitious or incompletely cited. Arranged under (1) Musical Works, (2) Literary Works, (3) Books and Pamphlets on Falla, (4) Book Chapters and Articles on Falla, and (5) Expositions and Literary Tributes. Includes reproductions of the covers of nineteen books on Falla.

*   Chase, Gilbert. *The Music of Spain.* 2nd rev. ed. New York: Dover, 1959. 383 pp.

Cited above as item 97.

383. Crichton, Ronald. *Manuel de Falla: Descriptive
      Catalogue of his Works*. London: J. & W.
      Chester, Ltd., 1976. 80 pp.

          The published works are arranged chrono-
      logically. Entries include dates of composi-
      tion, performance, and publication, orchestra-
      tion, duration, and a brief history of the work.
      Synopses are provided when appropriate. List
      of unpublished works is incomplete and several
      of the dates given are incorrect. For example,
      Trois mélodies were first performed on 4 May
      1910, not "late in 1910." Also contains a bio-
      graphical note and the most comprehensive list
      of transcriptions and arrangements to date.

*   Demarquez, Suzanne. *Manuel de Falla*. Preface
      by Bernard Gavoty. Paris: Flammarion, 1963.
      252 pp.

          Cited above as item 66.

*   Falla, Manuel. *Spanien und die neue Musik: ein
      Lebensbild in Schriften, Bildern, Erinnerungen*.
      Translated and edited by Jacoba Grunfeld. Zü-
      rich: Verlag der Arche, 1968. 184 pp.

          Cited above as item 293.

*   Franco, Enrique. "Falla, Manuel de." *New Grove
      Dictionary of Music and Musicians*. Edited by
      Stanley Sadie. London: Macmillan, 1980. 6:371-
      74.

          Cited above as item 152.

*   Jaenisch, Julio. *Manuel de Falla und die span-
      ische Musik*. Zürich: Atlantis Verlag, 1952.
      184 pp.

          Cited above as item 71.

384. Marsh, Robert Charles. "A Selective Discography
      of Manuel de Falla." *High Fidelity* 7 (July
      1957): 63-66.

          Includes extensively annotated entries
      for each of Falla's major compositions.

*   Mila, Massimo, ed. *Manuel de Falla: con saggi
      di Melchior de Almagro San Martin et al., e
      scritti di Manuel de Falla.* Translated by Mario
      Bortolotto et al. Milano: G. Ricordi & Co.,
      1962. 362 pp.

          Cited above as item 347.

*   Molina Fajardo, Eduardo. *Manuel de Falla y el
      "cante jondo."* Granada: Universidad de Granada,
      1962. 250 pp.

          Cited above as item 75.

385. Odriozola, Antonio. "Las grabaciones en discos
      LP de seis grandes figuras de la música con-
      temporánea: Ravel, Falla, Bartók, Stravinsky,
      Prokofiev y Hindemith." *Música* 3-4 (January-
      February 1953). 61 pp.

          An early discography of long-playing rec-
      ords.

INDEX OF PROPER NAMES

References to entry numbers are in roman type. Page numbers are in italics.

AUTHOR INDEX

*References to entry numbers are in roman
type. Page numbers are in italics.*

Ager, L., 274
Aguilar, P., 93
Alberti, R., 132
Alejandro, L., 357
Altermann, J.P., 133
Amestoy, S., 209
Ansermet, E., 210
Antoine, R., 211
Ara, P., 358
Arizaga, R., 58
Aubry, J., 134, 135, 182,
    183, 275
Auric, G., 136

Bal y Gay, J., 137
Barce, R., 212
Beardsley, T., 184
Benedito, R., 314
Bilbao Aristegui, P., 261
Blas Vega, J., 382
Boas, R., 213
Bramanti Jaúregui, E.,
    34, 138
Bucher, F., 214
Buckle, R., 94

Budwig, A., *39*, *40*, *41*,
    42, 59, 185, 215
Bustos, J., 296

Campoamer González, A.,
    5, *10*, *33*, *42*, 60
Campodónico, L., 61
Cárner, M., *37*, 95
Carr, R., *41*
Casanovas, J., 62
Casella, A., 96, 216
Castillo Puche, L., 359
Chase, G., 97, 139, 217,
    262
Chiesa, Hector, 315
Chueca Goitia, F., 140
Claudel, P., *33*, 98
Cobb, C., 99
Collet, H., 360
Costas, C.J., 63
Craft, R., 126, 127
Crichton, R., *19*, *36*, *37*,
    64, 263, 383
Cúllar, J.M., 65

INDEX OF COMPOSITIONS
AND ARRANGEMENTS BY FALLA

*References to entry numbers are in roman
type. Page numbers are in italics.*